Samuel R. Pattison

Gospel Ethnology

Samuel R. Pattison

Gospel Ethnology

ISBN/EAN: 9783337285364

Printed in Europe, USA, Canada, Australia, Japan

Cover: Foto ©Lupo / pixelio.de

More available books at **www.hansebooks.com**

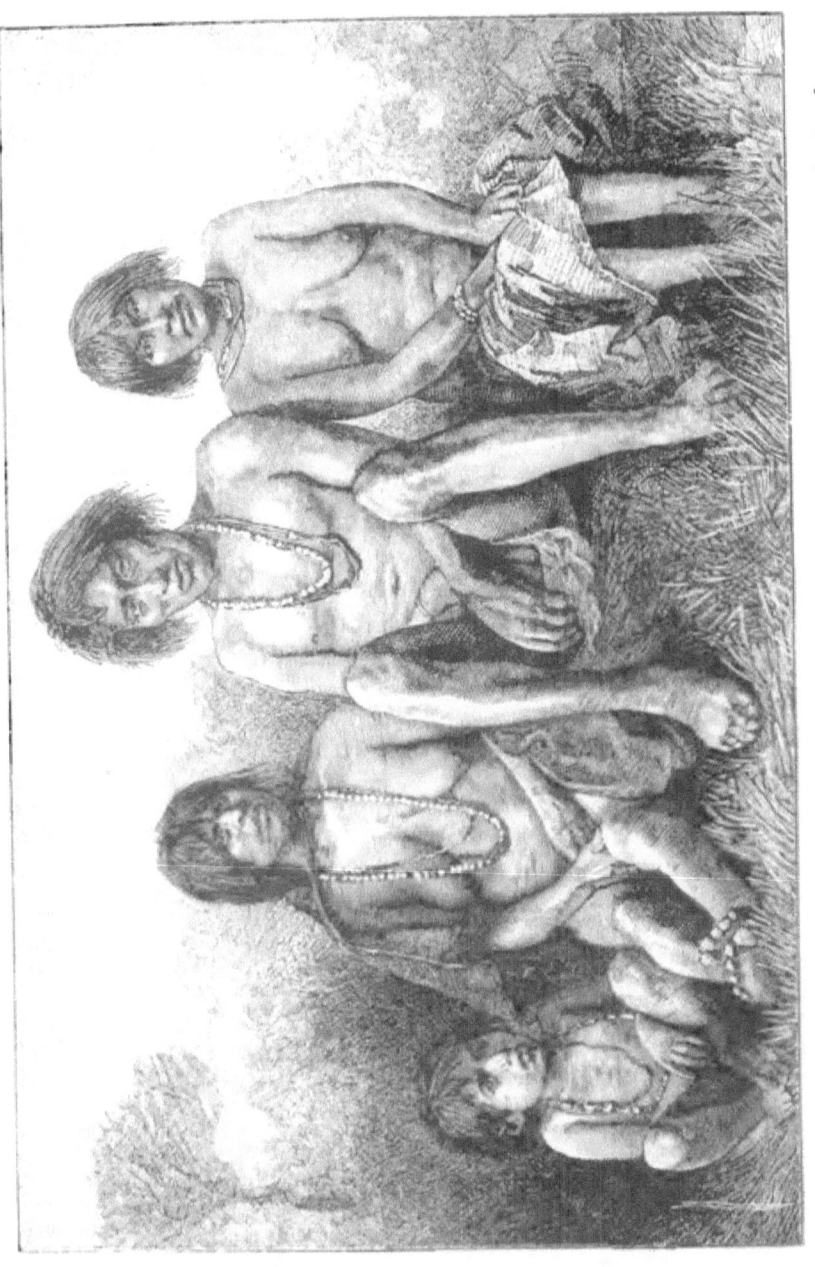

A GROUP OF PATAGONIANS.

See p. 128.

By S. R. PATTISON, F.G.S.
Author of 'History of Evangelical Christianity,' &c.

A NEW GUINEA NATIVE

NEW AND CHEAPER EDITION

THE RELIGIOUS TRACT SOCIETY
56 Paternoster Row 65 St. Paul's Churchyard
and 164 Piccadilly

"A gleam, a guess, which penetrated not
The long lone darkness which o'erhung that land
Of wonder and of loneliness, where once,
Amid the clusters of its marble shrines,
Man's sorrowing search for something to fill up
The blank within his soul found resting-place
In the cold worship of the unknown God.
There was a fire upon the altar there
Of Pallas, ever burning up to Heaven;
But no one knew its meaning. There was blood
Of consecrated victims,—sprinkled blood
And outpoured wine, and holy festival;
But no one guessed their import, for the light
Was but a spark, which glimmered and was gone."

HORATIUS BONAR.

CONTENTS.

CHAPTER I.
The Question Stated   PAGE 11

CHAPTER II.
The Physical Oneness of Man   15

CHAPTER III.
The Spiritual Oneness of Man   21

CHAPTER IV.
Ethnology   29

CHAPTER V.
The Black Races of Man Accepting the Gospel.—
    1. Negroes   41
    2. Kafirs...   48
    3. Hottentots   . 58

CHAPTER VI.

THE YELLOW RACES ACCEPTING THE GOSPEL—

	PAGE
1. Chinese	62
2. Japanese	69
3. Coreans	77
4. Burmese	78
5. Indian Hill Tribes and Aborigines	81
6. Malays	87
7. Malagasy	88
8. Papuans	91
9. Australians	95
10. Sandwich Islanders	97
11. Polynesians and Melanesians	98
12. New Zealanders	105
13. Mongols and Mongoloids	109
14. Lapps, Finns, Eskimos	112
15. American Original Races	119

CHAPTER VII.

THE BROWN AND WHITE RACES ACCEPTING THE GOSPEL—

1. Hamites	134
2. Semitic Races—	
(1) Jews	136
(2) Syrians	138
3. Kurds and Arabians	140
4. Abyssinians	143
5. Berbers	143

CONTENTS.

	PAGE
6. Nestorian Syrians	146
7. Armenians	148
8. Persians	151
9. Hindus	157
10. Slavonians, Russians, Basques	174
11. Scandinavians and Teutons	181
12. English	187
13. Kelts	193
14. Greeks	196
15. The Latin Races	197
16. French	205

CHAPTER VIII.

Conclusions and Summary ... 212

LIST OF ILLUSTRATIONS.

	PAGE
A GROUP OF PATAGONIANS	*Frontispiece.*
A NEW GUINEA NATIVE	*Title.*
A WOMAN OF SOU'LOU	10
BEDOUIN ARAB AND EGYPTIAN FELLAH	20
A MONGOL TYPE	29
BISHOP CROWTHER	40
A CONGO NATIVE	47
ZULUS	49
A ZULU NATIVE PREACHER	56
A CHINAMAN OF HIGH RANK	63
COREAN MANDARIN	76
MALAY TYPES	86
A HOVA—MADAGASCAR	89
A MOTU NATIVE—NEW GUINEA	94
A CIVILISED AUSTRALIAN LUBRA	96
A CIVILISED AUSTRALIAN ABORIGINAL	96
A MAORI CHIEF	105
A MONGOL LAMA	108
LAPPS	113
NORTH AMERICAN INDIAN	123
AN EGYPTIAN FOOTMAN	132
ABYSSINIAN BOY	142
A SYRIAN PATRIARCH	145
AN ARMENIAN FAMILY	147
A PERSIAN LADY	153
A NATIVE OF NORTH INDIA	159
INDIAN SNAKE CHARMER	163
A HINDU WOMAN	167
A HINDU BEARER	170
A NATIVE HINDU PASTOR	172
A NORWEGIAN PASTOR	184
A GREEK WOMAN	195
FRENCH TYPES	206

A WOMAN OF SOULOU.

GOSPEL ETHNOLOGY.

CHAPTER I.

THE QUESTION STATED.

> Thus 'mid the ruin sin has wrought
> In things without, and inward thought,
> Through the dark world of sin and pain
> Some shivered fragments still remain;
> Some fragments, which to heathen sight
> Present that vision of true light
> Which in the Christian's sky above
> Shines like the sun—that God is love.

MOST of the observed facts of humanity have been copiously described by the numerous writers and students who in recent times have given much attention to these subjects. The morals, superstitions, and even the religions of mankind have been abundantly investigated and illustrated; but I am not aware that the nature of the reception which has been given to revealed Christianity has been formally treated, and I venture to think there is still room for an exposition of the place which the Gospel holds in relation to ethnology. The response which the Divine revelation of the Gospel finds in human nature can be ascertained from the experience and testimony both of missionaries and of historians. If it were found that this response was in any sense a partial one, if restricted to certain races, if mankind as a class, either cultured or savage, rejected Christianity as utterly foreign to its needs, we must look elsewhere for proofs of its Divinity. But if, on the contrary, the glad tidings of salvation through Jesus Christ, heralded by type and prophecy in the Old, and fully revealed by its Living Author in the New Testament, have been received wherever they have been presented and explained, by people of every tribe and class with eagerness and assent, then we may be justified in regarding these announcements as the Divine truths which they claim to be, and as 'worthy of all acceptation.'

From the day of Pentecost downwards, the divine life, the life of regenerated man, has shown itself to be independent of all the divisions of ethnology, and proved its paramount claim to be 'the power of God unto salvation unto every one that believeth,' as it proclaims to all the world, 'God commandeth all men, everywhere, to repent.'

Some opponents of missions say it is absurd to suppose that the same ideas which are applicable to the accomplished European can be at all suited to the degenerate African. They further say, 'If your religion were the product of infinite wisdom, it would be provided with a different Gospel for every different race of mankind.' Had it been left to mere geographers or ethnologists to determine the missionary's destination, they would have warned him off from the fierce Zulus and the miserable Fijians, from the Torrid and from the Arctic regions, as alike hopeless and incapable of improvement. Microscopists tell us that all human blood is precisely identical in its composition, and just as there is not one race adapted to the air and another to the water, so in spiritual things there is not one race requiring a provision of salvation different from another. The Gospel of Christ has scored its triumphs in every field, and has proved in a new and large sense the truth of the proverb, 'Man's extremity is God's opportunity.'

We do not propose to give either a history or an account of Christian missions in general, but to select representative instances of acceptance of the Gospel by all the races and nearly all the families of mankind. It is obvious that for this purpose the date of occurrence is immaterial. An instance from the earliest annals of the Church is as valuable as one from the latest. The whole missionary story is an uninspired continuation of the Acts of the Apostles.

We are particularly favoured, as Englishmen, with materials for the prosecution of this inquiry. By our Colonies we are brought into the knowledge of people possessing the utmost variety in race, climate, civilisation, and habits of mind and life.

It may be observed that the proposition now under consideration is not affected by the variations of Christian doctrine within the pale of evangelicalism. However the terms of the foundation dogma of the Gospel may be expressed or construed, the fact of its universal acceptance remains. Nor do we rely on any analogy or secondary sense in regard to this, but on the simple truth urged on the motley population of Rome by the Apostle Paul, for 'the free gift of God is eternal life in Christ Jesus our Lord.'[1]

The more complete becomes our intercourse and the more frequent our communication with the people of foreign lands, the stronger becomes our persuasion of the solidarity of man. We find that equally in spiritual as in intellectual, moral, and physical things, man is linked to his brethren. This is the assumption of St. Paul in his Epistle to the Romans, it is the verdict of history, the basis of jurisprudence, and underlies the whole doctrine of redemption.

[1] Romans vi. 23 (R.V.).

CHAPTER II.

THE PHYSICAL ONENESS OF MAN.

> Children are we all
> Of one great Father, in whatever clime
> His providence hath cast the seed of life,
> All tongues—all colours. Neither after death
> Shall we be sorted into languages
> And tints—black, white, and tawny, Greek and Goth,
> Northmen and offspring of hot Africa.
> The all-seeing Father,—He in whom we live and move,—
> He the impartial judge of all—regards
> Nations, and hues, and dialects alike.
> According to their works shall they be judged,
> When even-handed Justice, in the scale,
> Their good and evil weighs. *Southey.*

It is calculated that the family of man, now living on the earth numbers about 1,450,000,000 of inhabitants, of whom 800,000,000 live in Asia, 320,000,000 in Europe, 210,000,000 in Africa, 110,000,000 in America, 10,000,000 in the islands of the sea.

In complexion the range is from white to ebon black, the proportion being five of the former to three of the latter, and there are 700,000,000 who are brown, yellow or tawny. It is estimated that 500,000,000 are clothed and live in houses, 700,000,000 in imperfect dwellings, and 250,000,000 are wandering barbarians.

As to religion, the 1,450,000,000 are divided as follows: 860,000,000 are pagan, comprising 600,000,000 Brahmans and Buddhists; 160,000,000 unclassified pagans; 100,000,000 Parsees, Confucianists, Shintoists, Jains and other smaller pagan sects; 410,000,000 are Christians, composed of 225,000,000 Roman Catholics, 75,000,000 of the Greek Church, and 110,000,000 Protestants; 172,000,000 Mohammedans; 8,000,000 Jews. The 860,000,000 pagans are found chiefly in Asia and Africa, and comprise 99-100ths of the population, with scattered millions in the Americas and islands of the sea. The 410,000,000 Christians are principally found in Europe and America, with a few millions in Asia, Africa and the Islands.

A small section of the 110,000,000 Protestants are acting on the persuasion that it is their function and duty to make known to all others the doctrines of Christianity, and to urge their acceptance. If, as we submit, it turns out on examination that the provision of the Gospel, both in substance and in mode, is precisely and exactly adjusted to a work which needs to be done, then we establish a scientific basis for missions which cannot be overturned, and we may claim for missionary objects and methods all the dignity of scientific work. To prove this we propose to refer to some leading facts in the science of man, and then collate these with the ascertained results of modern discovery and Christian missions.

The existing differences between the races of mankind are so considerable, and yet their similarity in other respects is so great, that the scientific world has for many years been divided into two opposing camps, on the question of their origin.

One party maintains that the indications prove a common descent from the same stock; the other asserts that the evidence requires the belief in several localised centres of origin. Dr. Topinard, in his *Eléments d'Anthropologie Générale*, a volume of nearly 1200 pages, maintains that not only are there no pure races upon the globe, all human groups being crossed and mixed, but race itself has no separate existence. It is, he says, merely the notion of a collection of characteristics or of an hereditary type in a succession of families; the origin of this hereditary type always escapes us. And therefore the ethnologist must content himself with inquiry into peoples, taking them just as they appear at the moment of observation. There are those who have maintained, as Agassiz did, that men were created in distinct races; but surely the identity of character which can be shown to subsist among them all, in regard to their chief features, is an unanswerable argument for the *unity* of the race, and its descent from a single pair. This conclusion the majority of ethnologists now hold to be established on strictly scientific grounds.

Mr. Edward Tylor, the accomplished author of the standard text-book on Anthropology, and the President of the Anthropological Section, at the meeting of the British Association in 1884, in his *Early History of Mankind*, after passing in review the long array of divers customs existing in the world, says 'The facts collated seem to favour the view that the wide differences in the civilisation and mental state of mankind are rather differences of development than of origin, rather of degree than of kind.' Dr.

Pritchard, in his *Physical History of Mankind*, at the close of a long and laborious statement of the facts, thus concludes: 'If the evidence adduced in the foregoing pages is sufficient to establish these conclusions which I have ventured to deduce from it, it may be affirmed that the phenomena of the human mind, and the moral and intellectual history of human races, afford no proof of diversity of origin, in the families of man, but that on the contrary, in accordance with an extensive series of analogies above pointed out, we may perhaps say that races so recently allied and even identified in all the principal traits of their physical character, as are the several races of mankind, must be considered as belonging to one species.'

Our limits will not allow of a full treatise on historical ethnology, and as every writer on the latter subject has constructed his own system, it is inevitable that there should be variances between our statement of pedigree and those of some others. The science is constantly being made more complete by the progress of discovery, and we can only claim to have constructed a provisional arrangement, which, however, will be found to include all the leading varieties of the race, and to classify mankind according to the best and latest authorities on the subject.

BEDOUIN ARAB AND EGYPTIAN FELLAH.

CHAPTER III.

THE SPIRITUAL ONENESS OF MAN.

> In such a quarrelling and tumult and jangling about other matters, thou mayest see this one by common consent acknowledged as law and reason, that there is one God, the King and Father of all; and many gods the children of God, and ruling together with Him—this the Greek says, and the Barbarian says, the inhabitant of the Continent, and the Islander, the wise man and the fool say the same.
>
> MAXIMUS TYRIUS, about A.D. 150.

WE have now to examine whether the unity of man extends to his religious faculties as well as to his physiological and intellectual conditions.

Three qualities appear in man, differentiating him from the rest of the animal kingdom.

First, a moral sense, an intuitive apprehension of a right and wrong.

Second, reflection, or the power of turning the moral gaze within.

Third, the possibility of raising himself above a law of absolute necessity.

We everywhere find him using these distinguishing faculties.

Religious sentiment, developed by the moral sense,

is universal. The testimony of geographical travellers and historians is unanimous in ascribing to man of every race the acknowledgment of some kind of supernatural power to be worshipped and propitiated. This unknown force above themselves has been personified by them in the grandest and most beautiful objects of the material world; they have, as is so accurately portrayed in Romans i. 23, 'changed the glory of the incorruptible God for the likeness of an image of corruptible man, and of birds, and four-footed beasts, and creeping things.'

The theistic statement of the old biographer, Plutarch, may still be adduced, after centuries of exploration and discovery: 'If one travel the world it is possible to find cities without wealth, without letters, without kings, without coin, without schools or theatres, but a city without a temple, or that with no worship, prayers, &c., no one ever saw.' The great tragedians of Greece expressed in their writings such presentiments of a Divine government, of the sinfulness of sin, and of the need of expiation, and breathed forth so pathetically the longing for reconciliation to God, that they have not inaptly been called 'the pagan prophets of Christianity.'[1]

The obvious inference from these facts is that there is a universal consciousness that God has dealings with men. Men are everywhere prepared for a revelation from God, not to reveal Him, for that is already written in our nature, but to teach us what we may expect from Him, and what is our duty toward Him. 'The recognition of religion itself (in distinction from

[1] See *Christ and the Heroes of Heathendom*, published by the Religious Tract Society.

the varied forms it may assume) as a natural need and tendency of the human mind, implies the reality of its object. Even if that sacred object should withdraw itself from our understanding behind an impenetrable veil, even then we could say nothing concerning it save this one word—" It is."'[1]

It is natural for man to look above himself to a mysterious and greater power, to whom or to which he may utter his prayers and offer his worship, but this worship is usually associated with fear and dread rather than love and adoration. It is only when he thinks he discovers sympathy in this power, and is able to personify and love it as manifested in the Divine Redeemer, that he can realise it as a living, renovating, exalting energy, worthy the name of religion.

We quote from Professor Flint, who says: 'The study of comparative theology is a magnificent demonstration, not only that man was made for religion, but of what religion he was made for. The more accurately the nature of religion is determined, the more thoroughly its various forms are studied, and the more closely they are compared, the more conclusively will it appear that Christianity alone is the ideal of all religion, and alone satisfies the spiritual wants of humanity, that Christ is the "Desire of all nations," and the appointed Saviour of the world, in whom all perplexities of the soul are reconciled, and in whom alone the restless heart of man can find peace.'[2]

We shall subsequently show by testimony that the revelation of Christ, as the giver of repentance and

---

[1] Reville, *Hibbert Lectures*, 1883.
[2] *Faiths of the World*, p. 431.

eternal life, meets these inherent wants of the soul. It turns the heathen's poetical dream of forgiveness and future bliss into a blessed reality. When received it is at once felt to be a new light and a new life. It shows us all things as we never saw them before. It suddenly fulfils a half-formed intuitive notion, converting it into clear and certain knowledge. A Divine atonement, peace through satisfaction of all claims against our moral nature, and love springing from thankfulness and joy,—these are its elements and its fruits. Love, grounded on a recognition more or less of the substitutionary death of Christ, develops the fact that under all the modifications which ethnology displays there lies in man a sensitiveness which corresponds with the great Divine light and love of the Heavenly Father. So everywhere man, under examination, discloses a sense of law, of sin, of responsibility, and a desire for forgiveness. He eagerly reaches forward to embrace the proffer of a sin-offering. Conscience seeks a moral refuge, not to be found in itself, and on a display of the work of Christ closes with it and accepts it on the ground of its aptness and sufficiency. This assent and acceptance is the soul's epoch, from the date of which Christ and His salvation are ours, and we are in sympathy with Him. Repentance and loving obedience are born twins. This is the simplicity that is in Christ. It is well expressed in D'Aubigné's definition of faith: 'The subjective appropriation of the objective work of Christ.' The great Christian Sacrifice draws all men to it.

The appeal of Christ in the Gospel is to the individual man. The conviction of sin is of course a personal thing; the exhibition of Christ's mediatorial work and sacrificial death, supplies and satisfies this personal need; and by the spontaneous acceptance of the Redemption man becomes not the less, but the more a man, for he has exercised his peculiar and sovereign power of determination, and this on the highest of all subjects. It is evident that God framed the soul of man to be a habitation for Himself, that such noble faculties as the understanding, will, and affections are far too good for any other guest. Sin has closed the doors against Him, but Christ comes there and knocks, waiting until the will brings Him the keys. He enters, and the usurper's possession is at an end. The rapid action and strong attachment of the Christian convert is not the result of a process of reasoning only, but the quick emotions of love and loyalty. 'Man feels that he was born for God, and looks for some sign to assure him of the reality of a fellowship with the unseen.'[1]

The scope of Scripture is the revelation of Christ, and it is to this that the soul is turned in conversion. The love of Christ supplies the needed motive and duty becomes the outworking of affection. The 'old man' both in the heathen and in the Christian world is supplanted by a new affection. The distinctive character of this state of things is, that it consciously springs from a man's own free choice. In the act of conversion from self to God, however brought about by power from on high, the happy subject feels that he is exercising a free choice, and therefore gains in dignity, and is not lowered in his own esteem, save towards God. The turning-point in these cases

[1] Westcott, *Gospel of the Resurrection*, p. 13.

appears to be the recognition of a loving personal God, instead of an exacting arbitrary power. Obedience at once becomes the offering of gratitude for favours received in redemption, and of admiration for the unrivalled excellence and loveliness of the Mediator. Directly the truth is apprehended that a Divine Being, who might have been self-devoted, chose not to be so, but rather to devote Himself unto death for us in sacrifice, love springs up.

This is the case everywhere. It is the beam of the Holy Spirit. Under His enlightening influences works of goodness follow, and holiness grows in the atmosphere of the Divine fellowship. The need of the soul is not only for saving truths, but for a higher life, and herein we are met by the ever available gift of God.

Man's conviction is, that happiness may be sought, but his experience tells him it is not to be found in nature. This is the case with which the Gospel deals. If, by a discovery, the mind can be brought into accord with a desire and capacity for attainable happiness, felicity is restored, the end of existence is attained and the whole creation becomes a harmony. A reception of the message of the Gospel, a belief in the fact that Christ came on earth, took our nature, suffered in our stead, produces love to Him ; and this, with the trust which it naturally draws forth, constitutes that cordial satisfaction in Him which is happiness and order.

Meditation and further instruction in the Word of God continually augment this acquisition, and the life becomes a life of growing trust and repose. This is the fruit of salvation, and it is often attained without any clear or enlarged apprehension of other questions or disclosures of religious truth. The great fact that in some way the death of Christ has been the means of reconciling us to God is sufficient for the peace of the soul. Until this is made known the mind is hopeless and confused. After it is revealed, all is gleaming with new light.

Love, worthy and pure, love, the 'greatest enchantment,' has changed the nature ; fear with its torments is banished. Through Christ we trust in God, and are complete in Him. We no longer live under a reign of selfishness, for we are not our own.

All this appears to be capable of being handled by reason. The ordinary laws of evidence and methods of induction surely apply, and we invite the scholar, as well as the man of business, to inquire into the case, and act as becomes the enviable possessor of the accumulated experience of the ages.

We may here give one fact as an illustration of our argument. It is well known that the Religious Tract Society of London acts on the principle of expressing in all its publications the doctrine of the way of salvation, through the truth applied by God the Holy Spirit. The Society grounds the sale of its publications on the demand for these truths in all quarters of the globe. If these doctrines were at variance with the common sense and common needs of humanity, the circulation of the publications must of necessity be small and transitory. But what is the fact? Now, in the eighty-seventh year of its existence under this law, we learn from the report for 1886 that demands for Gospel teaching have arisen and been supplied in 181 languages and dialects. Of these, about seventy are read by the Indo-European or Aryan races, eighty by Mongolians and thirty-one by the various brown races.

As the result of modern observation we affirm that just as there has been found no tongue so barbarous as to be incapable of expressing a translation of the Gospel, no utterances too rudimental to form syllables of divine truth concerning Christ, so there has been found no individual heathen so dark, brutish, stolid, and degraded, as to be incapable of being made a new creature in Christ Jesus by the grace of the Holy Spirit.

The sentiment of ethnological unity in connection with the person and work of Christ, is finely described by the late Cardinal Wiseman, in his lectures on the connection between science and revealed religion.[1] 'And truly when we see how He has been followed by the Greek, though a founder of none among his sects, revered by the Brahmin, though preached unto him by men of the fishermen's caste, worshipped by the red man of Canada, though belonging to the hated pale race, we cannot but consider Him as destined to break down all distinction of colour and shape and countenance and habits ; to form in Himself the type of unity to which are referable all the sons of Adam, and give us in the possibility of this moral convergence the strongest proof that the human species, however varied, is essentially one.'

[1] P. 167

A MONGOL TYPE.

CHAPTER IV.

ETHNOLOGY.

> They say His doctrine spreads from land to land,
> It softens stony hearts and joineth hostile hands,
> And buildeth up in loving hearts a realm of peace.
> FRITHIOF SAGA.

THERE are two ways of regarding the facts of ethnology: either by beginning with the Scripture account of the races of mankind dealt with in this and other histories, or by surveying the actual facts, and classifying them as they now stand. We intend to use both methods, but only to the extent sufficient to ground the argument of the present work.

It is natural for a Bible reader to inquire for the tripartite division indicated in the account of the three sons of Noah—Shem, Ham, and Japhet. Scripture follows down the fortunes of the families, but gives almost exclusive attention to the line of descent of the family of Abraham, and all others only incidentally come into the view. In a general way we may affirm that these three families subsist in well-marked distinction at the present day, and roughly correspond with leading divisions which have been established on the ground of scientific observation alone.

In a general way it is often said that Europe represents the posterity of Japhet, Asia of Shem, and Africa of Ham. This is a very rude classification but we will, under the guidance of Canon Rawlinson, set forth how it is made out, and for more specific information refer to his work *The Origin of Nations*. Corresponding to this is the existence of three families of speech:—1. The Aryan or Indo-European, to which Latin, Greek, Persian, Sanscrit, Keltic, Slavonic, German, English, and most modern European languages belong. 2. The Semitic, comprising Hebrew, Phœnician, Armenian, Arabic, Assyrian, and Ethiopian. 3. The Turanian, embracing the Finnic, Hungarian, Tartar, Turkestan, Mongol, Indian Hill-tribe tongues, and Tamil.

Following our authority and referring to it for the evidence, we must assume that the descendants of Japhet (Genesis x. 2) were and are (1) the Indo-Persians and Aryans; (2) the Kelts; (3) the Teutons; (4) the Græco-Italians; and (5) the Slavs.

The descendants of Ham (Genesis x. 6) were and are the Ethiopians or Northern Africans, the Egyptians, the Nubians, and the Syrians.

The descendants of Shem (Genesis x. 21, 22) were and are the Hebrews, the Persians, the Assyrians, and the Lydians.

Professor Sayce, in his short treatise on the ethnology of the Bible contained in the *Handy Book for Bible Readers*, carries on the descent of the primæval post-diluvian families down through the ages until the Christian era, and traces the original stock into the peoples of the world at the time of our Saviour.

Leaving the histories for the present, we will briefly consider the facts as they appear visually to us. Looking at the varied ethnological maps of the whole world, we have to note that no two writers adopt precisely the same system, as their knowledge of distinctions and languages is at present continually enlarging; and therefore the reader may find the following divisions somewhat different from those to which he has been accustomed. Suffice it now to say that they have not been adopted without careful examination of the most recent, though often conflicting, authorities.

The divisions into which writers on ethnology separate the human race are mainly three: the Black, the Brown, and the Fair. But out of these numerous subdivisions are formed. Ethnologists agree for the most part in the grouping of the races, but differ only in their pedigree and relations.

Opportunities for observation, photographs, portraits, illustrated books of travel, and the description given by experts,[1] have familiarised us with the forms displayed by most of these groups, and we may conveniently class them as follows :—

I. BLACK,—ARTHOCHROI.

1. Negroes and Central Africans.
2. Kafirs.
3. Hottentots.

II. YELLOW,—MESOCHROI.

4. Chinese, Japanese, Coreans.
5. Burmese, Siamese, Karens, Assamese.
6. Hill tribes of India, Tamils, Telegus, and Singhalese.
7. Malays.
8. Papuans, Australians, Malagasys.
9. Polynesians, Melanesians, Mikronesians.
10. Mongoloid northern races, Finns, Lapps, Eskimos, Samoyedes.
11. American Indians, North and South America.

III. BROWN AND WHITE,—LEUCOCHROI.

12. Hamites, Egyptians, Gallas.
13. Semitic races, Jews, Arabians, Abyssinians, Nestorians, Armenians.
14. Aryans, Persians, Armenians.

---

[1] Peschel's *Races of Man*, H. C. King and Co., 1876; Professor Flower's *Address to the Anthropological Institute;* Dallas, *Primary Divisions of Mankind, Journal of the Anthropological Institute*, February, 1886, p. 366; Reusch, *Nature and the Bible*, Clark ed. (translation), 1866; Professor Flower, *Journal of the Anthropological Institute*, May, 1885, with other very numerous manuals and monographs.

15. Hindus, Scindians.
16. Slavonians, Russians, Basques.
17. Scandinavians, Teutons, Bohemians, English, French.
18. Greeks, Albanians.
19. Latins, Italians, Spaniards, Portuguese.

With regard to the antiquity of these distinctions, Mr. E. B. Tylor, in his inaugural address to the Ethnological Section of the British Association, 1884, referring to the first inhabitant says:—'The evidence of caverns such as those of Devonshire and Perigord, with their revelations of early European life and art, has been supplemented by many new explorations, without shaking the conclusion arrived at as to the age known as the reindeer period of the northern half of Europe, when the mammoth and cave-bear, and their contemporary mammals had not yet disappeared, but the close of the glacial period was merging into times when in England and France wild men hunted the reindeer for food as the arctic tribes of America do still. Human remains of these early periods are still too scarce and unsatisfactory for determining race-types.' After much discussion amongst the learned, the present opinion of anatomists is that the most ancient skulls do not essentially vary from modern forms.

Race divisions are by no means absolute, and every year the progress of commerce, civilisation, and religion renders them less so. It is calculated that in Germany only sixty-two per cent. of the population are Germans, in France only ninety-three per cent. are French, in Russia seventy-eight are Russian, and so on. The variety of language is greater even than that of territory.

At a meeting of the London Anthropological Institute held May 25th, 1887, Mr. R. S. Poole read a paper *On the Egyptian Classification of the Races of Man*. This was based on the famous tablets of the four races in the tombs of the kings at Thebes, B.C. 1400–1200.

The types were:—

1. Egyptian, red.
2. Shemite, yellow.
3. Libyan, white.
4. Negro, black.

By comparison with monuments of the same period and with some of earlier date, we learn that the first race, clearly an intermediate type, is seen to comprehend the Phœnicians, the Egyptians, the people of Arabia Felix, and those of the opposite coast. The Libyan race included an aquiline type with supra-orbital ridges, and receding foreheads, as well as a straight-nosed type. These two types inhabited the south-west of the Mediterranean, and some of the islands. The Negro race included the Negro and Nubian types. The Hittites and Hyksos, or shepherds, belonged to that great empire, the Hittite, which for so long a period entirely disappeared from history and knowledge.[1]

Three facts need to be borne in mind during the consideration of the subject. First, that differences in all the divisions are transmissible and interchangeable. Secondly, that there are numerous exceptions

[1] See *Fresh Light from the Ancient Monuments*, by Professor Sayce.

in each class, showing the probable reversion to some type common to all. Thirdly, that the mixtures between these races are so extensive and numerous as to render absolute subdivisions only approximately true.

The actual condition of things in regard to race is unstable as a whole, though the facts are sufficient to establish the general grouping above indicated as a truth of natural history. There is evidently everywhere a capacity for change more or less from one form into another, but the divisions are founded on resemblances of easy and familiar application.

Professor Flower says:—

'The difficulty of parcelling out all the individuals composing the human species into certain definite groups, and of saying of each man that he belongs to one or other of such groups is insuperable. No such classification has been, or indeed, can be obtained. There is not one of the most characteristic, most extreme forms, like those I have just named, from which transition cannot be traced by almost imperceptible gradations to any of the other equally characteristic, equally extreme forms. Indeed a large proportion of mankind is made up, not of extreme or typical, but of more or less generalised or intermediate forms, the relative number of which are continually increasing, as the long-existing isolation of nations and races breaks down under the ever-extending intercommunication characteristic of the period in which we dwell.'[1]

We therefore with confidence speak of the distinctions broadly historical both in race and language,

[1] *Nature*, 1885, p. 362.

which enable us to treat the Jews and Arabs, for instance, as Semitic races,—the Indian and European and Persian races as Aryan, from Iran, the region where we lose them on the line of ascent to Japhet,—and the Mongols and American Indians and Polynesians as Turanians—*i.e.* nations outside of the Aryans.

We have briefly indicated under each heading some results of examination into the question of origin.[1]

The same high authority pronounces :—

'After a perfectly independent study of the subject, extending over many years, I cannot resist the conclusion, so often arrived at by various anthropologists, and so often abandoned for some more complex system, that the primitive man, whatever he may have been, has in the course of ages divaricated into three extreme types, represented by the Caucasian of Europe, the Mongolian of Asia, and the Ethiopian of Africa, and that all existing individuals of the species can be ranged around these types, or somewhere or other between them.'[2]

Evidence is wanting to trace down through the ages and over the globe, the stream of population. The bifurcations and the flow have often gone on without external record ; owing too to the recurrence of type in individual cases among all people, and still more to the intermingling which has taken place by conquest and colonisation, and by intermarriage on the borders, the task has become more and more difficult. Yet it is not hard to say that the mass of

---

[1] See particularly Mr. Loring Bruce's *Manual of Ethnology, The Races of the Old World*, Murray, 1882.

[2] *Journal of the Anthropological Society*, May 1883.

any particular people bear characteristics of origin, or that traces, principally of language, are extant in history whereby we may fairly conclude the course of progressive population.

The key to a large portion of ethnology is to be found in the rise and progress of the Indo-European race of which we in England form a part. In early days this became divided into Asiatics and Europeans. The Sanscrit Hindu races are the main branch of the Asiatic Aryans; the Persians and Western Asians, including Armenians, constitute another branch extending into Europe.

The European Aryans separated into two branches, north and south, the Sclavonians forming the one, and the Bosnians, Servians, and Bohemians, diverging into Goths, Scandinavians, and Teutons, on one hand, and into Greeks and Latins, with the Kelts, on the other, together forming the peoples of modern Europe.

At the date of the first promulgation of Christianity, the peace of the Roman Empire had occasioned a vast and continuous flow of different nations towards the centres of commerce and of empire. It was to these that the early preachers of the Gospel opened their world-wide commission. They spoke to the divers nationalities which thronged the streets and market places of Antioch, Athens, Corinth, Ephesus, Alexandria, and Rome. They nowhere complain that their message was unintelligible or repugnant to the moral nature of their hearers.

Tertullian, writing two centuries after the first promulgation of Christianity, remarks on this characteristic. He says, 'The Moors and Getulians of Africa, the borders of Spain, several nations of France, and parts of Britain inaccessible to the Romans, the Sarmatians, the Dacians, Germans, and Scythians and other countries belong to Christ.'

The report of the Church Missionary Society for 1886 thus summarises the modern facts:—

'We see abundant fruit granted to the Society's direct missionary labours in the heathen and Mohammedan world: baptisms of adult converts which are of special interest—the first-fruits at Mpwapwa and Uyui, the first-fruits from among the Aino aborigines of Japan, the first convert from Mohammedanism in Egypt, the second convert from among the Gónds of Central India, a fakir and poet in Bengal, five lepers in a leper asylum ; a leading Hydah chief in Queen Charlotte's Island, seventy years of age ; and nearly one hundred persons from a hitherto untouched community of despised and out-caste Punjab villagers.'

In the great drama of history all the considerable nations have in turn played a part ; and in the presence of the Gospel of Christ all diversities disappear, and 'They come from the east and from the west, from the north and from the south, to sit down in His kingdom.'

BISHOP CROWTHER.

CHAPTER V.

THE BLACK RACES OF MEN ACCEPTING THE GOSPEL.

I. THE NEGRO.

IN now presenting proofs in detail we take the order previously indicated. The presence of the negro constitutes one of the most difficult problems of ethnology. His home is in the intertropical belt of the Dark Continent, including Guinea, the large basin of Central Africa, Western Soudan, and the Mozambique. By importation in modern times he is also established in the southern portions of the United States of America, in Brazil, and in various islands in the wide Pacific. His physiognomy is so strongly distinctive, that if anywhere on earth a radical difference in the stocks of mankind can be established, it should be here. The woolly hair, projecting muzzle, flattened nose, and round eyes, mark him off from all other races. There are, however, throughout the Dark Continent negroid races possessing these characters in very varying proportions.

The religion of the negro consists in a dread

of evil beings, whom he seeks to propitiate by sacrifices and charms, and under whose influences he supposes himself continually to dwell. He is somewhat slow and dull in mind, but quick in emotion, affectionate and faithful, naturally imaginative, susceptible, and religious. Is he the pure descendant of a black variety, or are the many coloured shades of his associates, approximations in a darkening process which has gradually become intensified?

The unchanged aspects of the ancient representations we have in the Egyptian wall-paintings 3,000 years old lead to the former conclusion, and the prevalent opinion now is that the negro is an original variety, allied to the Hill tribes of India, to certain black races in China and Burmah, to the Andaman Islanders, and to the Papuans.

But whatever may be the ethnological embarrassments the Gospel finds no difficulties. Before the revelation of a Divine Saviour the identity of the black and white races becomes a magnificent truth. The charge of inferiority on the part of the black races, which was once a commonly received opinion, is even now occasionally made. But modern observation and experience confute it. The qualities evinced by the dark races in their struggles for freedom show that their low mental status is simply the result of centuries of adverse circumstances and sufferings, which other centuries of an opposite character will assuredly efface. It was only in 1807 that negro slavery was abolished in British possessions, and all other European nations have been ever since with more or less reluctance following the example of England in the career of emancipation which obtained its crowning victory in the United States in 1863.

With regard to the moral nature of man, observers have failed to establish any radical difference between the dark races and others, whilst the records of the various missionary societies prove their equal susceptibility to the claims and culture of Christianity.

There is no mysterious innate tendency in the savage races to dwindle and disappear before the civilised white man, although such an effect has undoubtedly been developed by the result of evil habits and disorders introduced by the latter. It will be the pride of Christianity to check and efface this baleful influence, and by the habits induced by its teaching to restore the coloured and barbarous races to their full rights.

Queen Candace's Ethiopian treasurer was doubtless an African, and the truth concerning the Lord Jesus Christ unfolded by Philip the Evangelist from the fifty-third chapter of Isaiah was the means of his conversion. His anxious and thoughtful soul answered promptly and effectively to the call of Divine love. The same voice can now call forth a similar echo, and the Scriptures are now circulated in forty-seven of the languages and dialects of the African races.[1]

On January 17th, 1758, Wesley was preaching at Wandsworth, and was heard by an eminent West Indian planter then seeking health there. The hearts of the planter and of two of his female slaves were touched by the words of the preacher. Wesley baptised the two slaves, one of whom, he says, was 'the first regenerated African he had ever seen.'

Catherine Ruyters, a Hottentot, better known by

[1] See Memorandum by R. N. Cust.

the name of 'Old Catherine,' and amongst the coloured people as 'Old Grannie,' died at Swellendam in South Africa on July 18th, 1848. She was at the least 110 years old. She was born in the district of Swellendam, and spent her long life entirely in that region, so that she was known to most of the inhabitants. In her younger days she lived in the darkest heathenism, and was altogether without God. But on becoming a servant in the family of a pious elder of the Dutch Church at Swellendam, she heard the Scriptures read, and became acquainted with the purport of the Gospel, and earnestly sought to receive and understand the love and worth of Christ. She was admitted by baptism as a member of the Church, being then upwards of a hundred years old, and maintained a consistent and pious deportment until her death. For her Christ was in the fullest sense 'All.' 'It was astonishing,' says the relater, 'to see how she became excited and affected when any one spoke in her hearing of His sufferings and death. This always seemed to agitate her entire soul. "For me, for my sins, He had to suffer all that," she would say, whilst frequently the tears flowed down her cheeks.'

A missionary of the Church Missionary Society writing about the recaptured negroes at Sierra Leone says: 'Their thirst for information is intense and ardent. There is a holy enthusiasm among them to read the Scriptures and religious books. They often apply for them, and on asking them what kind they require, their reply is, "About God who so loved the world that He gave His only begotten Son, that whosoever believeth in Him should not perish but have everlasting life."'

A black nurse on board a West Indian packet was observed to be quite composed during a great storm, and on arriving at Plymouth her mistress requested a clergyman who came on board to ascertain the grounds of her composure. The negress attributed it to her faith in Christ. The end of the conversation was as follows:—

'How long is it, Ellen, since you first knew the Saviour, who is so precious to you?'

'Why, massa, some time ago, me hear Massa Kitching preach about de blessed Jesu. He say to me, "Black people, de blessed Jesu come down from the good world. He pity we poor sinners. We die, or He die, He died dat we no die. He suffer on de cross. He spill His precious blood for we poor sinners." Me feel me sinner, me cry, me pray to Jesu, and He save me by precious blood. Oh, Jesus Christ very good. He save me.'

The Rev. W. A. B. Johnson gave the following among other instances of the simplicity of the Christian negroes under his care at Sierra Leone. At one of their Saturday evening meetings, a man said:—

'By and by you talk about the Lord Jesus Christ. Him the doctor for heartsick people, oh, them words make me glad! You talk plenty about the medicine He give, and that He take no money, He give it freely. Oh, massa, that make me so glad! That time me go home me comfort very much. Thank God the Lord Jesus Christ gave His own blood for medicine, and take all my sins away.'

In 1849 Mr. Saker baptised the first Dualla convert in the Camaroons river, a true witness to the love and grace of the Saviour.

The history of missions to the African population of the globe, both in their native homes and in slavery in the West Indies, and the Southern States of America, is one continuous record of the correspondence between the negro mind and the Gospel. A Guinea negro, in relating his experience, observed, respecting himself, that from the time he came from the Guinea coast 'him no able to take a word, if any one offend him, me take knife, me take tick, me no satisfy till me drink him blood; me now able to take twenty word. Den me tief, me drink, bery bad ting me do. Somebody say, me must pray, me say no. Me say, Give me something good for eat, dat better than pray.'

'What made you change your mind then?' asked the missionary.

'Massa, me go to church one Sunday, an me hear massa passon say, "Jesus Christ came and pill Him blood for sinner." Ah, something say, "You hear that? Him pill Him blood!" Ah, so! Den me the tinner, me de tief, me de drunkard. Him pill Him blood for Guinea neger, oh, oh! Jesus died for poo' neger fore he know Him!'

Mr. Burchell asked a negro named Peter if he loved Jesus Christ to which he answered,

'Massa, me love Christ? Dat me do to me very heart.'

'But how do you know that you love Christ?'

'How me know? Massa, Christ no de Son of God? Him no come into dis world and pill Him blood for poor negro? How me know me love Christ? Who me love, if me no love Him? Who won't love, if Him no won't? Me love Him. Massa, me feel it, dat me know.'

An old negro in the West Indies, residing at a considerable distance from the missionary, but exceedingly desirous of learning to read the Bible, came to him regularly for a lesson. He made but little progress, and his teacher, almost disheartened, intimated his fears that his labours would be lost, and he said to him, 'Had you not better give it over?'

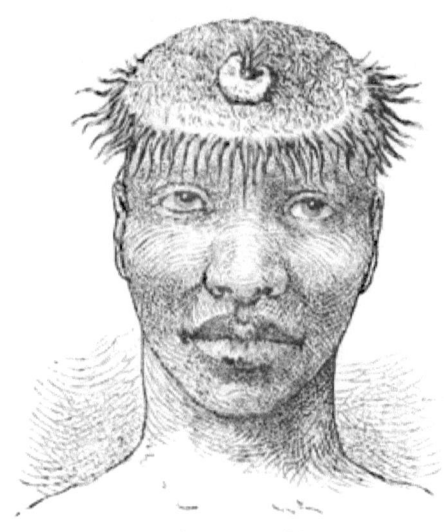

A CONGO NATIVE.

'No, massa,' said he with great energy, 'me never give it over till me die;' and pointing with his fingers to John iii. 16, 'God so loved the world, that He gave His only begotten Son, that whosoever believeth in Him should not perish, but have everlasting life,' added with touching emphasis, 'It is worth all the labour to be able to read that single verse.'

Nor need it be omitted that in the person of Bishop Crowther, of Sierra Leone, we behold a man, once a captive slave, a degraded heathen, now a native negro Anglican bishop, governing a negro church, with native negro teachers instructing native negro children.

A missionary on the Congo writes thus of his people:—

'How I wish you could see the people at the services—see their bright faces as they listen to those wonderful words of life, and truth, and love, hear their earnest prayers, listen to their heartfelt praises, witness the confessions of their past sins, and behold their joyful professions of their faith in Jesus and love to God; and you would thank Jehovah for His grace, and glory in His mighty power. There is no need for one to ask who are the converted and who not; for the joyous face and freedom of manner of the one, and the hopeless expression and slavish deportment of the other, make the contrast indeed great.'[1]

2. THE KAFIRS.

The Kafirs are black-red in colour, have woolly hair, and noses not flattened like that of the negro. They inhabit the south-east of Africa, and are intermediate between the black and the brown people. They are a numerous and wide-spread people, comprising four divisions—(1) the Amapondas and Southern Kafirs, (2) the Zulus, (3) the Eastern Kafirs, (4) the Bechuanas and northern tribes. They possess considerable aptitude for investigation, and are keen and even metaphysical in mental habits. The religion of the Kafirs familiarises them with the idea of prayer, sacrifice, propitiation, the supernatural, and a future life.

[1] *Illustrated Missionary News*, February, 1887.

ZULUS.

Their superstitions are innumerable. They worship a Supreme Being, and believe in the immortality of the soul, and in the efficacy of prayer—so far the requirements of the Gospel were not new to them; but their religion was one of fear, as their gods were in reality regarded by them as demons.

Dr. Livingstone, in his encounter with new tribes of barbarians on the great African rivers, says, in speaking of his intercourse with them, 'I pointed out in, as usual, the simplest words I could employ, the remedy which God has presented to us in the inexpressibly precious gift of His own Son, on whom "the Lord laid the iniquity of us all."' No one will say that the veteran explorer was not an expert in adapting means to the end in view.

A Zulu, over twelve years of age, who had heard the Gospel preached in Natal, and accepted it gladly, was warned against going back to Cetewayo's dominion with his profession of religion. He nobly replied, 'that he feared not death if he could learn more of such love as that of the Saviour.'

So advanced are the South Africans that there is a native undenominational Kafir missionary society in Kafirland, having for its object the evangelisation of all who speak the Kafir tongue. One of their requirements is that at intervals men should volunteer to go forth as evangelists and teachers. These should be of sound health, animated by glowing love to the Lord Jesus Christ, and intense compassion for the souls of those who are in ignorance; men who, having counted the cost, and ready, if need be, to remain till death at the post to which they may have been appointed.

Livingstone, when amidst the Makololo, writes in

his journal:—'Sunday, 12th of June. A good and very attentive audience. We introduce entirely new motives, and were these not perfectly adapted for the human mind and heart by their Divine Author we should have no success.'

A Kafir who had heard a missionary preach on the wrath to come was much troubled in mind, though he did not understand fully the meaning of the language. He was therefore brought to the Rev. Mr. Hood, from whom he obtained more just views of his lost state, and asked what he must do. Mr. Hood preached to him Christ crucified as the Saviour of sinners. The Kafir listened with eagerness, and fixing an anxious eye on the preacher, said:—'Sir, I am old and stupid, tell me again,' and, being told again, the tears rolled down the sable cheek of this man of noble and athletic frame, and he confessed his astonishment at the love of God, and the compassion of the Saviour. What is this but the same emotion which filled the heart of the dying Rutherford when he said, 'I want nothing now but a fuller revelation of the beauty of the unseen Son of God'?

In the year 1869 Moshesh, the great Basuto chief, who ruled over Basutoland for upwards of sixty years, and who, from his high intelligence, had favoured the introduction of the French Protestant Mission into his country, while sinking from age, but still bright in intellect, voluntarily declared his acceptance of Christ. The pastor who attended him says that the two ideas that specially struck him were 'a heaven opened to a sinner, and a Saviour who puts us in possession of it.'

Another chief, Moletsam, was converted about the

same time, and said, 'The Spirit of God has broken the hardness of my heart. My conscience has been troubled; I recall to myself the number of my sins, rapines, murders, adulteries. Now I am converted, Jesus is my Saviour.' The missionary says, 'He beams with delight when we present to him the promises of grace.'

Miss Sturrock's school at Peel Town in Kaffraria shows the saving impression of Gospel truth in the sable countenances of Hottentots, as well as of Kafirs, Fingoes, Negroes, and all varieties of the South African races. She writes: 'I could name one, and another, and yet another, who have passed away rejoicing in the blood-bought salvation, and resting firmly on the Rock, Christ, and dwelling now in His presence in glory.'[1] The following extract from a letter recently received from Miss Sturrock[2] will best add to the testimony we are adducing:—

'Towards the end of the last week in January we heard of the serious illness of a young man of about twenty years of age, who lived in one of the huts at a short distance from our "Home." On Sunday morning, the last day of the month, I went with Maggie (my interpreter) to visit him. On entering the miserable dwelling, the home where God was not known, where father, mother, and children had alike rejected and slighted the message of salvation, by the wall near the door, stretched on a pallet, I found the object of my visit. The hollow cheeks, sunken eyes, and short, hacking cough, unmistakably bespoke the near approach of death. I saw at a glance that his days

---

[1] Brown's *History of the Propagation of the Gospel*, ii. 459.
[2] *Our Work among the Kaffir Girls*, 1884.

on earth were near a close. He had been a wild, careless boy, and at first when I spoke of his state, my heart ached to see the absence of sorrow or repentance for sin.

'I did not disguise the fact that his end was near, and that soon, very soon, he would have to stand before his God—alone. He gradually became interested, and at last raised himself in a sitting posture as if to hear better. His look became troubled, and as I repeated the solemn words, "Prepare to meet thy God," he broke into an agony of tears and cries for mercy. His whole frame shook with agitation, but as I read one after another of the precious promises of pardon and forgiveness, he became quiet, and listened with eager attention. I felt that my prayers were heard, and that the eyes which had long been blind to a Saviour's love were about to be opened. At last I turned to Revelation xxii. 17, and the words there brought life to the dead. It was read in Kafir, and he asked to have the verse repeated. The second time he joined in the words, "Whosoever will, let him take of the water of life freely." I shall ever remember the change in his countenance as time after time he slowly repeated the word "freely"— and as if in answer to some one speaking to him he said, "I have come—Sam has come." He had indeed taken hold of his Saviour, and from that time it was all sunshine in his soul. He lingered for a fortnight after that Sunday morning, and during that time I visited him twice, sometimes thrice, a day. He suffered much toward the end, and often when scarcely able to speak I heard in broken whispers, "O Lamb of God, Sam's Jesus, stay with me!" His death-bed was a wonder to all who visited him, especially to his heathen friends, who could not understand his peace of mind and fulness of joy when almost on the brink of the grave. He always looked forward to our visits, and one afternoon a few days previous to his "going home" I had been detained until past my usual time. On his inquiring the reason, I explained that I had been detained speaking to a heathen girl, who for the first time had heard of the love of Jesus. I said that she seemed hardened, and unable to realise that He had died for her. With the light of his newly-found joy beaming from his eyes, he turned to me with these words: "Why did you not tell her that the Spirit and the Bride say, Come? She must believe that."

'Through sleepless nights and weary days of pain the name of Jesus was ever on his lips, especially for his godless father and others who were dear to him One day, on being asked the cause of his happiness he answered, "Why do you ask? do you not know that Christ is with me?" He frequently repeated (in his own language) Isaiah i. 18, "Come now, and let us reason together, saith the Lord: though your sins be as scarlet, they shall be as white as snow; though they be red like crimson, they shall be as wool." On the evening before he was called away he seemed to be suffering more than usual, and as I prayed with him he held my hand tightly clasped in his. Seeing that the end was so near, and that possibly I might not meet him on earth again, I repeated the words of David: "Though I walk through the valley of the shadow of death I will fear no evil." In a faint voice came the response: "Yes, He is with me; the Lamb of God is with me; I will fear no evil." When I was leaving him he pressed my hand to his burning lips, whispering, "Good night; I will meet you at the gate."

'Early next morning we received the tidings that he had gone—gone from a bed of pain and a

A ZULU NATIVE PREACHER.

comfortless home to inhabit one of "the many mansions;" to be "for ever with the Lord."'

In the Matabele country one of the agents of the London Missionary Society, Mr. Carnegie, writes of the natives of the town of Ingobie and the surrounding villages:—'They listen very attentively—some eagerly—to the old, old story of Jesus and His love.

The records of the recently-planted mission in Central Africa already contain numerous instances of the acceptance of the Gospel by people of wild tribes, to whom it has for the first time been made known. Alas, that we should here, as elsewhere, have to seek for our proofs amidst tales of cruel martyrdom and fierce persecution! The strength of personal attachment to the doctrines of salvation through the work of Christ has been tried in a fearful manner at Uganda, and has triumphed. Writing in June, 1886, Mr. Mackay, of the Church Missionary Society at Uganda, says:—'It is now a full month since the bloody persecution of Native Christians began. Those who were at the capital, and best known, were of course first arrested. About a dozen were butchered at once. Several were mutilated (Asiatic manner) afterwards; many were speared or otherwise killed in the endeavour to capture them in various parts of the country; while thirty-two were burnt alive in one huge pyre, after having been kept prisoners over a week.'

Writing on July 12th, 1886, Mr. Ashe says:—'Most of our work is now carried on in secret and under the cover of darkness. At first, when the storm broke upon us, all was darkness and fear. We knew the slaughter had been terrible, but who the slain were we knew not. After a while, at dead of night, one well-known face was joyfully welcomed, and then another. Soon many came, and with thankful hearts we found that though many had fallen, many, many more had escaped and are now hiding. On June 30th Bekwe-yamha, the young chief whom I mentioned of the royal family of Unyoro, came, as also an old reader named Lukai, and were baptized ; also a boy named Mudembuga, who is a very earnest little reader, and would have been baptized some months ago, but was hindered from coming on the day fixed.' The same letter contains the account of other baptisms, making twenty-three in all *subsequent to the massacres*.

3. THE HOTTENTOTS.

The Hottentots are a peculiar people by reason of their low development and inferior characteristics, contrasting strongly with the fine, handsome tribes amongst whom they live. They have a dark yellow complexion, prominent eyes, and hair like that of the negroes, and characteristics both of the Mongol and negro, yet differing from both. Their religious ideas are of the most meagre kind. They are found at the southern extremity of Africa, and were named Bushmen by the Dutch. They have been considered to be the most degraded of mankind, and we proverbially style them so, and use their name as a synonym for stupidity and mental deficiency. Dr. Pritchard says : ' It is indeed surprising, after all that we have heard of the sloth and brutal sensuality of the Hottentots, to learn that no other uncivilised race has given a more willing ear to the preaching of Christianity, and that none has been more strikingly and splendidly impressed by its reception.'[1] In the annals of the London Missionary Society we read that at the beginning of the Mission to Bethelsdorf, 'Many of the poor Hottentots were brought under

[1] *Physical History of Mankind,* i. 183.

deep concern for their souls, and appeared to be subjects of Divine grace.' Of some of these it may not be uninteresting to give a short account.

'Cupido, previous to his conversion, was perhaps as notorious a sinner as was ever known. He was infamous for swearing, lying, and fighting, but especially for, drunkenness, which often laid him on a sick-bed, as he had naturally a feeble constitution. On these occasions he often resolved to abandon that infatuating vice, and to lead a sober life, but no sooner did health return than he was again led captive by it. Sometimes, however, he was afraid of the anger of God, and being apprehensive that his wickedness would at length prove the ruin of his soul, he inquired of all he met by what means he might be delivered from the snare of drunkenness, imagining that after he had abandoned that it would be an easy matter to forsake his other sins. Some advised him to apply to the witches and wizards; but these proved miserable comforters, for they told him that his life was not worth a farthing. Others prescribed various kinds of medicines to him, but though he eagerly took them they also proved of no avail. He was at length providentially led to Graaf Reinet, where he heard Vanderlingen declare in a sermon that Christ Jesus was able to save the guilty from their sins. On hearing these glad tidings he said to himself: "That is what I want, that is what I want." His convictions of sin were afterwards greatly increased by means of a discourse by Dr. Vanderkemp. All his evil deeds seemed now to rise up in array before him; every word of the sermon, he thought, was directed to him, and as he continued to attend on the means of grace.

the secrets of his heart were still further manifested, and he was at length obliged to exclaim: "This is not of men, but of God." He now became earnest in seeking after an interest in Christ, and was exceedingly zealous in leading others to the same refuge.'[1]

A scene worthy of being represented by a painting was that recorded by Mr. Moffat as displayed at Cape Town, when the well-known and formerly dreaded Namaqualand chief, Africaner, first went down after his conversion to Cape Colony in spite of a large reward offered by government for his head. He there met Bend, the Griquan chief with whom he had previously had many a conflict, but who had also become a convert. The meeting of these two ancient foes, now brothers in Christ, was a remarkable occurrence, even in a history abounding in marvels.

When the missionaries entered upon their work among the Bushmen in Cape Colony, they laboured to convince their hearers by arguments addressed to their understandings, but their endeavours in this way were attended with little success. The savages continually raised objections to what was said, and it was often no easy task to answer them to their satisfaction. The missionaries then had recourse to that method which in the days of the Apostle Paul, as well as in modern ages, has been found the most effectual means of converting not only the heathen, but equally so the more highly-cultured races. They insisted chiefly on the dying love of Christ, and in a simple and affectionate manner they represented Him as an all-sufficient Saviour for lost and helpless sinners; they earnestly invited them to come to Him, that

[1] Brown's *History of the Propagation of the Gospel*, ii. 427.

they might be saved. The Hottentots who attended upon their ministrations now became interested, and perceived more and more the truth and excellency of the Gospel, which they found to be the power of God to their salvation.

The Rev. Barnabas Shaw records that on the 16th of October, 1823, whilst on his journey through Namaqualand, the following incident occurred: 'During the day an old Mozambique slave came up to our waggon and asked for a Dutch hymn-book. On asking if he could read, he took a small school-book out of his leathern sack and read, "For God so loved the world, that He gave His only begotten Son, that whosoever believeth in Him should not perish, but have everlasting life." The circumstance being very surprising to me, I inquired by whom he had been taught to read. He said, "My master some time ago hired one of your Namaquans to take care of the sheep. When he came amongst us we knew nothing of God or prayer, but he commenced singing hymns, and praying with us every evening. He then read out of the book, and told us of Jesus Christ. The words which he preached were so good to me that I longed to read them for myself. He was willing to teach me, and gave me his books. But his hymn-book is old and torn so that I can hardly read it. I long for another. Our teacher has gone away from us to the station, yet we still sing and pray together every evening."'

CHAPTER VI.

The Yellow Races Accepting the Gospel.

> Should bright'ning hope, to cheer the troubled day,
> Pour through the gloom a transient ray,
> Fate comes, and o'er the darken'd scene
> Spreads the deep horrors of its dreary reign.
>
> EURIPIDES, *Orestes*.

1. THE CHINESE AND THE CENTRAL ASIANS.

It cannot be denied that our next group of witnesses, the Mesochroic (mixed colour) races, comes from a people altogether different from the black races in aspect and external character; the great yellow races, Mongols and Mongoloids, comprising all the Chinese population, the Central Asians, Mongolians proper, and the northern races of Lapps, Eskimos, and the tribes of Northern and Eastern Siberia. They have for the most part high cheek bones and flat faces, obliquely set eyes and a yellowish green complexion. The Chinese and Tartar Mongols display forcibly the leading characteristics of the yellow race. They constitute the populous communities of China, Burmah, Siam, and Thibet.

The Chinese differ in language from every other

A CHINAMAN OF HIGH RANK.

race, and hence their language is supposed to have been suddenly arrested in its course of development, and its imperfections petrified, as it were. In physical appearance they are Turanians. Chinamen are beginning to be well known out of China proper. They are constantly extending over the islands of the Pacific, and in the American mainland. Their chief characteristic has been their stationary civilisation, a *status quo* of at least 4000 years' continuance. In religion they are chiefly Buddhists. The disciples of Confucius come the next in number. Confucianism has unquestionably been of immense service to China. It abounds in good precepts, but it is wholly wanting in sufficient motive for virtuous conduct, which only the religion of Jesus Christ supplies. The Confucian sentiment of justice or right is notoriously inadequate; it affords no stimulating energy, and is too tame and dry for human nature as it is. Taouism, another leading Chinese creed, is mere rationalism. Morality, grounded on selfish motives, and the promotion of selfishness in every possible form, constitute the basis of all these Pagan religions. We need not point out how these are exactly the opposites of Christianity, and, therefore, the success of the latter can in no way be founded on the doctrines or practices of the former.

Here, as in other cases, the faith of the Gospel comes in as an expedient unknown to nature, 'By a new and living way.' In the Report of the British and Foreign Bible Society for 1884 we read, 'A poor Tartar was turning over the leaves of a Tartar Testament, the Armenians around him were speaking depreciatingly of it, but he gave no heed to them, saying "Christ, I suppose, came to the world for us also

Every word of the Gospel is worth a thousand roubles."'
Take a recent instance from China. We are told that a China woman, Yaka, who had read and learnt about Christ as the Saviour of men, went to another village where her friends lived, and expounded the Scriptures, and preached Christ to them, so that they believed and burnt their idols and ancestral tablets, and set up a Christian meeting. Is not this Ephesus over again?

Another instance—'I am addicted to every sin you can imagine,' said Lin Kise Shan; 'I am an opium smoker, a libertine, a gambler, a drunkard, an unfilial man, and everything that is bad. Can Christ Jesus save me?' He had strolled into the chapel at Hankow. The preacher said 'Yes.' They prayed, and speedy conversion followed, and Lin, now over fifty years old, is the centre of a Gospel work in his own locality, where previously he was a notorious libertine.

This is an instance of that which most frequently occurs in conversion. The sudden discovery of the completed work of Christ affects the mind like a wonder of nature. It is as though a confused and difficult problem, on a subject of absorbing interest and of whose explanation we have come to despair, should all at once be simply solved by a new and unanswerable process.

The result in the mind is not only satisfaction, but joy, gratitude, and devotion, for the solution discovers to us a personal God and Saviour. However philosophic and abstract the missionary may be, yet his hearers receive Christianity, not as a dogma, but as a fact presented in the life and work of Christ. It comes not as a new doctrine, but as a new fact, not as a truth to be understood as proved, but as a Divine Person to be loved and therefore obeyed.

One of the agents of the National Bible Society for Scotland writes:—

'Among the converts there is one concerning whom I should like to tell you something. This man's name is Yang. He was a priest of Buddha for many years. Some years since he was seen pretty often at our chapel in this city, listening very attentively to the preaching, and apparently becoming more and more interested in the truth. Ultimately Yang became impressed with a sense of his own darkness and sin, and his need of a Saviour. He had many difficulties to contend with, and we were doubtful as to whether he would have sufficient courage to take the final step. At last he broke through all obstacles, cast aside his priestly robes, and turning his back on the 'Light of Asia' became an open disciple of our Lord Jesus Christ.'[1]

On Christmas Day, 1883, there was baptised at Pekin a well-to-do Chinese farmer. Upwards of a year before he had obtained a copy of the New Testament and of the *Peep of Day*. He mastered the leading truths of the Gospel, and under the address of an earnest simple colporteur was led to own the Lord, and become a true follower of Christ.'

The results of the mission of the London Missionary Society at Tientsin have been the acceptance of the Gospel by great numbers, and the establishment of churches and schools. One of the converts, a man of independent income, and of a naturally stubborn temper, but overcome by grace, goes up and down the

---

[1] *Religious Tract Society Report*, 1884.

country proclaiming everywhere the forgiveness of sins in the name of Jesus, and has been the means of planting the Gospel in several villages.[1] The female mission there has been very successful. Mrs. Lance writes :—'They are much disposed to gossip, and when they come to see me, it is something in the sermon, or in the Sunday school lesson, or a word about what God is doing for them or others, which is the most frequent topic of conversation. The Gospel of Christ has become so much to them that of Christ they cannot but speak.'[2]

The evangelisation of China is being effected greatly through native agency. There are already very numerous ordained pastors, colporteurs, Bible-women, theological schools and students, all natives. In 1886 Dr. Mills writes as follows :—

'I write this from an inn at a country village among the hills, sixty miles south-east of Tungchow. Five years ago this spring I visited this place for the first time, and stopped at this same inn, occupying the very room I do now. One morning I was having prayers with my assistant, Mr. Lan, when a man about sixty-five entered the room, and, greeting us very cordially, expressed his great satisfaction at meeting a minister of the Gospel, which he had long desired above all things. I asked him to join us in our reading and prayer, which he did, and afterwards told us his story.

'He said his name was Sun Hyoa Yang; he lived in this village, which is called Tong Kin Puh, and had a vegetable garden. Several years before (I think eight)

---

[1] *Report of the London Missionary Society*, 1886, p. 47.
[2] *Ibid.* p. 53.

a man passed through the district selling Christian books. For a few cash, less than a halfpenny, he had bought a little tract of a few pages. I think it must have been Dr. Martin's *Paul's Discourse at Mars' Hill*. He was led to buy it by the unusual clearness of the type. He read it and was interested. Others in the region had bought larger books, and from them he got, I think, the Gospel by Matthew, the Gospel by Luke, the Acts and Romans. He read the Gospel history as far as the crucifixion, and threw aside the book in disgust. "I will read no more," said he, "of a Man who could work miracles, but who hadn't spirit enough to defend Himself when spit on and abused." But the story had a strange charm for him. He read it again carefully. At last he got to understand the vicarious nature of Christ's suffering, and then his admiration and gratitude knew no bounds. He resolved to serve this Saviour, who for our salvation was buffeted and spit upon, and nailed to the cross.'[1]

2. THE JAPANESE.

These are the descendants of a primitive Turanian race modified by Chinese conquests. They are less Mongolian in appearance than the Chinese, and more like the Europeans. The Americans began the mission work here, declaring and expounding the doctrines of the Gospel. The recent rapidity of the intelligent and hearty reception of these truths throughout Japan, shows unmistakably the suitableness of the Divine remedy there. At first so great was the distrust of

[1] *Illustrated Missionary News*, 1886.

foreigners, and especially of Christianity, that at the end of five years there was but *one* baptised Japanese, and at the end of twelve years but ten. The first church was organised in Yokohama, March 10, 1872, and consisted of eleven members. There are now at least 11,000 baptised Protestant Christians, gathered into 150 churches. We find Independent Churches, Home Missionary Societies, Young Men's Christian Associations, Chautauqua Circles, and all forms of Church life and work. Theatre lectures on Christian themes, sometimes before immense audiences, are common and popular. The New Testament is translated and widely distributed. The Old Testament is in a form of Chinese which can be read by scholars; about two-thirds of it being also translated into Japanese and published. There are seven religious newspapers and periodicals; also a few hundred different tracts and other Christian books. The Evangelical Alliance of Japan has issued the statistics of Protestant missionaries in that country for 1885. There were 110 male missionaries (81 American, 19 English, 6 Canadian, 4 Scotch), and 74 ladies besides the missionaries' wives (67 American, 3 English, 3 Canadian, 1 Swiss). There were 165 "organised churches" or congregations, of which 57 were wholly, and 101 partially, self-supporting. The total membership was 11,678, and in 1885 there were 3,234 baptisms. Of the Native Christians, 4,800 were Presbyterians, 3,450 Congregationalists, 2,270 Methodists—most of these belong to American Societies; about 1,000 are connected with the Church of England and the American Protestant Episcopal Church.

In reading the following account of a Mission in

one of the islands of Japan, it must be borne in mind that the effort is entirely that of voluntaries who have embraced the religion of Christ, and therefore we confidently adduce it in aid of our argument.

'In 1882 a colony of Japanese Christians was founded in the island of Yezo (now called Hokkaido), the northern portion of Japan. The leaders, Messrs. Sawa and Sudzuki, were led to their Christian faith through the teachings of the late President Clark, who aided in the formation of the Agricultural College at Sapporo. These colonists were visited, in 1883, by the Rev. O. H. Gulick, of the American Mission in Japan, who has again visited them, and in a letter dated Urakawa, June 28, 1886, sends the following interesting particulars as to their welfare:

'"The original Christians in this colony are mostly from Sanda and Tamon (the branch church of Kobe) and from the Kobe church. These are the very churches with which the most of the direct missionary work that my wife and I have been able to do has been connected. Urakawa is the point I visited three years ago—one year after the founding of the colony.

'"Saturday, the 26th, was the first day of the feast. It was a reminder of what I witnessed in my youth, and of the Hawaiian quarterly communion season or the later time meetings of local associations, to see the people on horseback gathering early, some of them coming fifteen miles: men and women, young men and maidens, children before and children behind the saddle, in twos and threes on the horses, and all dressed in their Sunday best; the maidens with red and blue crape in their hair, and many with red in their belts. Then the horses picketed about the church, and an occasional yell from some war-horse who is snorting and pawing for a fight with a stranger horse, though not a devotional sound, is not an unfamiliar accompaniment of such a religious festival.

"'Among the exercises of Saturday forenoon was the reading of the call for the council which this body of Christians had sent to thirty-one Congregational churches of Central and Southern Japan, and to the Methodist church of Hakodate, the Presbyterian church of Hakodate, and to the independent body of Christians at Sapporo. Mr. Harada responded as the delegate sent from the three churches of Kobe, Tamon, and Hiogo. The afternoon services consisted of a sermon by the missionary, the reading of creed and covenant, questions and assent of members, prayer for the church, ordaining prayer and laying on of hands upon Mr. Tanaka, a charge to the pastor and a charge to the church; then the reading of letters of congratulation from the Sanda and Tamon churches, the former comparing the action of the Urakawa settlers to that of the Puritan Fathers. On Saturday evening eighteen candidates for baptism were examined by the missionary and delegate. On Sabbath morning we had a sermon by Mr. Harada, the baptism of the eighteen persons by the young pastor, followed by the Lord's Supper. Sabbath afternoon Mrs. Gulick held an interesting prayer-meeting with the pastor's highly-educated wife (a graduate of the Kobe Girls' School) and the women of the church. A prayer-meeting, attended by twenty-five persons, at a later hour closed this most interesting series of services.

"Thus this young church in the wilderness, 180 miles east of Hakodate, starts off with thirty-three members all in the prime of life; a pastor of their choice, who is a graduate of an agricultural college, able to read English, and one who has had some experience in evangelistic work in connection with the Kobe church, and who has an excellent, educated wife, also a reader of English; a church-building capable of seating 150 persons, and all paid for."[1]

A Japanese missionary tells of a poor woman who had tried to win salvation by making and consecrating a garment. It was made of white linen, and written all over with 'sacred words,' or extracts from their sacred writings. It is commonly believed that if such a garment be worn at the time of death the wearer will be sure to go to heaven. This poor woman, being anxious to secure her title to heaven, had made journeys to many priests, and each one, after writing certain passages on the garment, had attached his seal, in order to certify its correctness. Thus equipped, the poor woman believed herself to be sure of heaven, but, greatly to her surprise, found that her conscience was still uneasy. After a while she heard the Gospel, and was led to renounce all dependence on the garment and to rest her soul on Christ. She would then have burnt the garment, but on her pastor telling her not to do so she gave it to him for a missionary museum.

A leader in a Japanese newspaper for the year 1875 runs thus:—'There is nothing better than Christianity to aid in the advancement of the world, but there are sects that are injurious, as well as sects

[1] *Illustrated Missionary News*, January 1887.

that are beneficial. The best mode, therefore, of advancing our country is to introduce the most free and enlightened form of Christianity and have it diffused among the people.'

It will not be denied that the *Pilgrim's Progress* is a book which derives its universal interest from its lively display of the peculiar doctrines of the Gospel. It follows that the fact of its acceptance is good evidence of the truth of our proposition that the great Christian tenets are in accordance with the nature, the constitution, and the experience of men. The report of the Religious Tract Society for 1886 thus refers to the translation of that immortal work into Japanese :—

'This work is now ready for publication. This glorious book has been an object of peculiar care to the committee. How carefully and prayerfully its translator, the Rev. W. J. White, has done his work, he alone can tell; but of one thing the committee feel assured, that the dear old pilgrim's English dress will never be shamed by the Japanese robes in which he is now wrapped. He goes forth upon his pilgrimage through this dark land equipped with everything that loving hearts could suggest. He has with him his beautiful Japanese pictures to show to delighted children; he has his thrilling tale of wonderful adventures with which to interest the young; and he has the deeper meaning of his life to unfold to those older ones who feel as he once felt, the burden of sin pressing heavily upon them.' The work has been widely accepted and sold in such numbers as to justify the expectations of its translators.

COREAN MANDARIN.

3. COREA.

On the recent opening of this hitherto secluded country to European influences, it was speedily discovered that its people presented no exception to the general desire for the grace and truth of the Gospel, when presented in 'the simplicity that is in Christ.' The first wave of spiritual religion which entered was in the shape of Scriptural tracts. We are told by Mr. Ross, of Mookden, that they are 'scattered over the greater portion of Corea. They have been sent into the capital, whence they have found their way to neighbouring cities and provinces. In still greater numbers have they been distributed over Western Corea. It is simply impossible for me to personally follow their course and see their work. But if I am to believe what I hear from all parts, their influence is nowhere wholly lost. A Corean mandarin from the capital is here, who informs me that there are "believers in all the provinces." Not long ago a young man was baptised here, who came from the very shadow of the pumice peaks of the White Mountains. From his home to this city is a distance reckoned at about 600 miles, and occupying a month of toilsome travel. Not very long ago two men were baptised here, who came, the one from the south of the capital, the other from the extreme north-east of Corea, who had walked 1,000 miles to get to Mookden.'

4. BURMESE.

The Burmese belong to the Indo-Chinese race. They are smaller and darker than the Chinese. They have made considerable attainments towards civilisation, but yet are most imperfect in their social and political life.

A correspondent of the *Times* (October 21st, 1886), who appears to have made a special study of Burmah, referring to the ethnology of that country, says that 'tradition points to three main streams of colonisation into Burmah. The northern sea-board, now known as Aracan, is said to have received its earliest population and polity from the Buddhist kingdoms of Bengal. The southern sea-board, or Pegu, with Rangoon as its modern capital, is supposed to owe its civilisation to settlers who crossed the sea from the Madras coast. The ancient kings of the inner country which we call Upper Burmah, also claimed an Indian affinity. But, as a matter of fact, they and their people poured across the mountains and down the river valleys from the confines of China and Mongolia. These three prehistoric divisions have left their mark on the political geography of Burmah at the present day. Each of them has in turn advanced upon and crushed its neighbours, while the whole has been from time to time submerged by fresh avalanches of wild races from the north and east.'

In June, 1819, Judson, the eminent American missionary, was cheered by the first application of a native Burmese to be received into the company of

Christ's believers. This man wrote a letter to the missionary of his own accord, in which he says:—

'I, Moung Nan, the constant recipient of your excellent favour, approach your feet. Whereas, my lords, there have come to the country of Burmah, not for the purpose of trade, but to preach the religion of Jesus Christ, the Son of the Eternal God, I, having heard and understand, am with a joyful mind filled with love. I believe that the Divine Son, Jesus Christ, suffered death in the place of men to atone for their sins. Like a heavy-laden man I feel my sins are very heavy. The punishment of my sins I deserve to suffer. Since it is so, do you, sirs, consider that I, taking refuge in the merits of the Lord Jesus Christ, and receiving baptism in order to become His disciple, shall dwell on with yourselves, a band of brothers, in the happiness of heaven?'

Myat Kyan, another convert, was a signal instance of the power and sovereignty of Divine grace, which chooses and moulds its subjects in a wonderful manner. He was by birth and religion a Buddhist, but being of an inquiring and thoughtful mind, he entertained strong suspicions that the religion of his ancestors was a baseless fabric. He sought for some creed on which he might more safely rest the interests of his soul, but he groped long in darkness. He first became the disciple of a Brahmin ascetic, and for two or three years practised various austerities, but he could not rest in these. He then said, 'There must be somewhere a revealed religion; I will inquire of the Mohammedans.' He had not then seen a Christian teacher, nor heard the name of Christ. He went to a mosque, and there heard of 'One God, and Mohammed His prophet.' The idea of one eternal, uncreated omniscient Creator struck his mind with great force A ray had broken through the clouds of heathenism upon his soul. He listened to the Koran, hoping to find there a system of morals by which he could obtain the Divine favour. But he was disappointed, and left the mosque determined to inquire further for a revelation of this Eternal Being. He next went a few times to a Roman Catholic place of worship. There he heard the name of Christ as a Saviour, but he was directed to pray to Mary, and Peter, and the other apostles, and an endless succession of saints. This seemed to him but another variety of heathenism, especially the worship of the Virgin, and he said, ' If I must worship a human being as God, I would rather worship Gaudama, a man, than this woman ; and as for Roman images, I cannot see that they have any more claim to Divine honour than Burman images.'

For a long time after this Myat Kyan was in a depressed state, till at length the troubles of war brought him and his family to Moulmein, an important station of the American Baptist Board in Burmah. Here he became acquainted with Dr. Judson, and listened to his preaching. Day after day he tarried at the place of worship from morning till night. One prejudice after another was removed, clouds broke away from his horizon—he *saw* and *felt* the truths of Christianity. The Holy Spirit had touched his soul with His quickening influences. He had discovered the pearl of great price, and he determined at any cost to secure it ; and he soon found that he must part with all he had to obtain it. His family and friends observed the change, and their hatred of Christianity was aroused.

His brother told him plainly that he would renounce him as a brother; his wife that she would abandon him if he was baptised; his two sons, and an adopted son, that they would no longer call him father. They made no ado when he turned ascetic, or was about to become a Mohammedan or a Roman Catholic; but that he should become a *Christian*, they could not and would not put up with. Nevertheless, he persevered, and became a distinguished and useful convert.

There are at present 350 Christian churches in Burmah, and nine-tenths of the work is carried on by converted native agents, chiefly among the Karens, who support their own Christian organisations for worship and education.

> 'How great the wisdom, power, and grace,
> Which in redemption shine,
> Angels and men with joy confess
> The work is all divine.'

5. INDIAN HILL TRIBES AND ABORIGINES.

There are many millions of these aborigines in India, divided into Kolarian and Dravidic races, who are still in physique, language, manners, and religion, absolutely different from the Hindustanees among whom they live. They are by Professor Frederick Müller divided into three great branches—(1) Dravidian branch: Kôls, Santhals, Bheels, and others; (2) Tamils, Telugus, Malyalians, &c.; (3) Singhalese.

Some embarrassment arises from the ethnological necessity for classing the long civilized people of

Southern India and Ceylon, speaking Tamil and Telugu, with the still wild Kolarians.

The hill tribes, the supposed aborigines of India, are Turanians. They are dark, with straight hair, small eyes, thick-limbed, and short in stature.

In 1799 Carey and Ward, on their way down the Ganges, made the first attempt to evangelise the Santhal and other aboriginal tribes during a visit to the Rajmahal Hills, round which the great Ganges sweeps.

'I long,' wrote Carey from this spot to his colleagues, 'to stay here and tell these uncultivated heathen the good news from heaven. I have a strong persuasion that the doctrine of a dying Saviour would, under the Holy Spirit, influence and melt their hearts.'[1]

It was fourteen years before the German Mission to the Kóls, the aborigines of Upper Bengal, the occupants of Chota Nagpore, produced any result. It was commenced by six disciples of Pastor Gossner in 1846, of whom only two remained to witness in 1850 the conversion of eleven of the race. Thenceforward success has been achieved in a wonderful manner, and now these interesting tribes are living in villages, forming a complete Christian community.

There are about 400 native preachers and teachers working in the cause of Christ among these tribes, the Kóls, and the Santhals.

Mr. Clarkson relates :—

'I had pitched my tent on the banks of the Nuya, amongst the Kóls, an aboriginal tribe reported by Montgomery Martin to be "savage and irreclaimable."

[1] Smith's *Life of Carey*, p. 120.

I preached day after day the doctrines of repentance toward God, and faith in the Lord Jesus Christ. These doctrines I illustrated in every way I thought adapted to reach the consciences of the people. One day after addressing them on these subjects I asked them:

'"Do any of you weep on account of your sins?"

'To my utter delight a young Kóli about twenty-two years of age, a farmer, said with considerable feeling: "I weep on account of my sins, ah! my eyes do not weep, but my soul weeps on account of my sins."

'I replied, "If so, what do you wish to do?"

'He said, "To believe in Christ."

'"What do you know of Jesus Christ?" asked I with intense interest.

'"I know that He died for my sins." That man was baptised and led a consistent life.'[1]

Dr. J. L. Phillips, of the American Baptist Mission, speaking, at the Calcutta Missionary Conference, of the lower classes and the aborigines says, 'Our books are sought with avidity, even the poor paying for them cheerfully; the sweet hymns of the Church in all ages are sung, and our Lord's Prayer daily and devoutly repeated, and not this alone, thank God! but our Sacred Scriptures in numerous vernaculars are eagerly studied by multitudes in the schools and in the houses from whence the people come. I should be delighted to speak of happy surprises I have had amongst aborigines and Hindus, revealing a fondness for God's Word, and real diligence in the study of it. I believe there are many that have their every hope of salvation in the atoning merits of Jesus' blood.'

The Gospel has continued to triumph among these

---

[1] Clarkson's *India and the Gospel*.

races under the work of those who have gone preaching only Christ crucified. This charm has opened a way as well into the hearts, consciences, and minds, of the Santhal peasant as into his semi-civilised Tamil or Telugu brother, and the still more polished Singhalese.

A Tamil native thus records his experiences in the last report of the British and Foreign Bible Society: 'When I was a heathen schoolmaster of a Tamil school on Feb. 1st, 1866, the late Rev. V. Védenâyagan gave me one of the New Testaments which the Bible Society had sent for heathen masters. For six years I studied this book, and many a time argued with Mr. Védanâyagan about the differences between Christianity and heathenism. At last the Lord who is rich in mercy opened the eyes of my mind and revealed to me that the Christian religion contains the way of salvation of souls. I itinerate through villages preaching the Gospel to the heathen.'

We may here mention the persevering efforts of the Basle Missionary Society among the various peoples in Southern India, now much mixed with the Hindus, but of Dravidian descent, speaking Maláyalim and kindred languages. Mangalore may be considered as the centre of this mission. The report of the Basle Mission for 1886 gives 1,999 as the number of church members, and says, amongst other instances of successful work:—'In Boomghatee there was a dispute whether the Christian or the Mohammedan religion satisfies the heart's craving. The superiority of the former was established before a well-behaved audience.'

MALAY TYPES.

6. MALAYS.

Malays are usually of medium height, olive yellow or brown in colour, with smooth black hair and scanty beards. They occur in typical force in the peninsula and islands of the Indian Archipelago. Murder, theft, and cruelty appear to have become naturalised amongst them. Another large and various branch of the Malays are the Eastern Polynesians, comprising the Maories of New Zealand, a fine race possessing more of the Caucasian than of the Mongolian features.

Great interest was awakened in 1839, and subsequently by the conversion of a Mohammedan at Singapore named Ali, who was employed as Malay teacher to the missionaries. He often expressed himself thus: 'The religion of Jesus is the only true one given to man, because it searches the heart and works that change in man *which the Koran, and the study I have given to it for twenty years*, could not produce.' In a letter giving his experience he says he was often constrained to exclaim, 'Who can cleanse me from these sins? Mohammed cannot cleanse me, how much less can my father and mother! In vain have I year after year learned the Koran, for it cannot deliver me from my sins. None but Jesus Christ can do this.'[1]

The population of the Straits Settlements consist of Malays to the extent of one half; the greater part of the residue are Chinese, and the balance East Indian. The aborigines are called Sakirs and Semangs, and lead a wandering life. Mr. Bruckner, of Samarang,

---

[1] *London Missionary Magazine*, 1840, p. 164.

wrote in 1849, that on a visit to Sourabaya, a number of natives had been spiritually awakened by reading tracts in Javanese. Their leader had sought and found the people who had issued the tracts, and obtained a New Testament which he read diligently, and so became a believer in Jesus. He repented of his sins and looked to Christ for pardon. 'They said they loved the Lord Jesus so much because He had loved them, and had even sacrificed His life for them.'[1]

7. MALAGASY.

The people of Madagascar, before the missionaries visited them, were to a considerable extent organised in government, and had many habits and institutions of civilisation. In religion they were addicted to witchcraft, to many degrading beliefs, and to the practice of human sacrifices. In the great persecutions aimed against Christian converts in 1849 the story of the Christian confessors was precisely that of the proto-martyr, Stephen. Faith in the atoning work of Christ was the belief which they had received, and would not give up for dear life. The fifteen who were executed by being thrown from the summit of the hill at Amparinana, and the four of high rank who were burned alive, sang of their faith in Jesus, and prayed for their persecutors till death closed their sufferings.

The whole story of the Malagasy persecution cannot be differentiated in motive from the recorded martyrdoms of the faithful followers of Christ in the first ages of Christianity. We may describe the

[1] *Jubilee Volume of the Religious Tract Society*, p. 506.

Malagasy, so far as our subject is concerned, in the words of the Apocalypse:—

'And one of the elders answered, saying unto me, What are these which are arrayed in white robes,

A HOVA—MADAGASCAR.

and whence came they? And I said unto him Sir, thou knowest. And he said to me, These are they which came out of great tribulation, and have washed their robes, and made them white in the blood of the Lamb. Therefore are they before the throne of God, and serve Him day and night in His temple: and He that sitteth on the throne shall dwell among them. They shall hunger no more, neither thirst any more, neither shall the sun light on them, nor any heat. For the Lamb which is in the midst of the throne shall feed them, and shall lead them unto living fountains of waters, and God shall wipe away all tears from their eyes.'[1]

A young man in Madagascar, who had warmly espoused the cause of the Redeemer, was observed by his Christian companions to shed tears at every mention of the name of Jesus. A missionary to whom this was mentioned took particular notice of the circumstance in subsequent conversation with him, and bore testimony to the fact. One of his Christian friends asked him one day how it was that his tears always gushed forth when he mentioned the name of Jesus. He replied, 'How can I do otherwise than feel, while I mention the name of that beloved Saviour who suffered and died on the cross for me?'

Faith in a sacrifice as a propitiation, is evidently based on universal intuition, and so the atonement revealed in the Gospel is everywhere intelligible.

Old Culverwell in his quaint style says, 'The poor remains of natural religion are the more striking in the barbarian than in the Greek; and hence we are often surprised at the prompt and full acknowledgment of revealed truth when it is once discovered by the former.'

---

[1] Revelation vii. 13–17.

8. PAPUANS.

These races, comprising the Papuans and the Fijians, are the inhabitants of the Australasian islands of the great Pacific. They are brown-black in colour, with crisp and frizzled hair, and are often called Oceanic negroes; until very recently they were all pagans and polytheists, believing in sorcery and holding the most rudimental conceptions of the supernatural.

The Fijians are probably the finest representatives of the Melanesians; but excepting among the mountain tribes, there is everywhere a considerable admixture of the lighter Polynesian race. Tonga and Samoa are inhabited by the brown Polynesian race, and contain perhaps its finest representatives. They vary in colour from dark to light bronze, are tall and well proportioned, with almost European features. But there are different types even among this isolated race; sometimes a Mongolian type appears, with a strikingly Japanese look. The Rarotongan, Hervey, and Loyalty islanders, belonging to the Polynesian race, are often employed as missionaries to the westerly "savage" Melanesians.

The mission work was begun in Fiji in the year 1835 by the Wesleyan Missionary Society. The islands were gradually, and in some cases rapidly, won by the influence of Christianity; but in the mountains of Na Vita Levu, heathenism remained till within the last seven years. At present, however, there is not a single professedly heathen village in the country; the whole of the group is nominally Christian, and nearly every village has its own church, resident pastor, and school. The distant island of Rotumah is also included in the Fiji Mission. A marked feature in the conduct of this mission is the large employment of native agency, local preachers, teachers, catechists, and ordained native ministers. The Fijians have the whole Bible in their own language, and they are great readers of it.[1]

In the life of John Hunt, the Lincolnshire ploughman, who became the Apostle of Fiji, translated the Scriptures into Fijian, and was a grand instrument in bringing the barbarous and cannibal people from the deepest darkness of heathenism into the glorious light of Christ, we read of a service held by the native converts in the early stage of successful mission work, and he tells how the *Te Deum* was chanted with noble reality. 'It was the victory song of redeemed souls; and the dark faces quivered with joy as they answered one another in that heathen land, saying, "We praise Thee, O God, we acknowledge Thee to be the Lord." But when they reached the words, "Thou art the King of Glory, O Christ!" voices failed, and streaming eyes and broken cries of "Jesu! Jesu!" lifted more eloquent praise to God.'[2]

It will surely be sufficient as a proof of our proposition in regard to Fiji, to quote from the catalogue of the Colonial and Indian Exhibition at South Kensington, 1886, the following extract, enumerating the books exhibited as current native literature:—

Rev. James Calvert:—
　　Bible in Fijian language.
　　New Testament in Fijian language.

---

[1] See *Handbook to Fiji*, Colonial Exhibition, 1886. For an admirable account of the effects of the Gospel in these islands see Miss Gordon Cumming's most instructive volume, *Fiji*, which furnishes a complete justification of missionary work.　　[2] *Life of John Hunt*, p. 184.

Genesis, Exodus, and Psalms, in Fijian language.
Hymns, Catechism, and Book of Offices, in the Fijian language.
Lessons on Gospel History in Fijian.
Outlines of Sermons in Fijian.
Church Service in Fijian.
Two Hymn Books in Fijian.
New Testament printed in Fiji.
Pilgrim's Progress in Fijian.
Daniel and Esther in Fijian.
System of Theology in Fijian.
Sacred Cards in Fijian, illustrated.
Rotumah New Testament in Rotumah language.
Missionary labours among cannibals.
Autobiography of a Native Minister in the South Seas.

The Papuans of many parts of New Guinea may still be described as inveterate cannibals, cruel and treacherous. They are impulsive and demonstrative. In their native religion they are polytheists. It is amongst these repulsive specimens of humanity that the missionaries of the London Missionary Society are now successfully introducing the Gospel.

The first of the Papuan youths who embraced Christianity was Wiru, a youth who had been taught by the Dutch missionaries in New Guinea. After some years of endurance of reproach for his fondness for the notions of the white man, he applied for baptism, saying, 'I desire to be baptised, for I love Jesus, He is my Saviour, and has ransomed me with His blood.' After further examination he was baptised, and the missionary says that during the ordinance his countenance seemed illuminated with 'the peace that passeth all understanding.'[1]

[1] *Illustrated Missionary News*, March 1st, 1879.

Mr. Chalmers, in his highly interesting book on *Pioneering in New Guinea*, gives the history of one of the renowned chiefs of the Motu tribe called Aruako. He says:—'When I knew him first he was a wild-looking savage, with the largest, longest, frizziest head of hair on the coast, or that I had

A MOTU NATIVE—NEW GUINEA.

seen in New Guinea. He in no way made any friendly advances to the missionary or teachers. His expression was sour and repellent, and gave the impression that he was always angry. He is about forty-five years of age, well-built, and about five feet eight inches in height. He used to punish the slightest insult to himself or his friends at once and satisfactorily, not by taking life, but by robbery. To make things worse, he was a man who believed much in witchcraft, and was full of superstition, the kind of man that any one would find it difficult to win over. He did not wish the teachers to remain, and would rather they left. A few years ago he began attending services, and soon took an intelligent interest in them, which grew into a desire to change his mode of life. He is now a reformed man. His fierceness of expression has gone, the determined look remains. He is a man of will, seeking to do right. He has become an active preacher of Christianity.'[1]

9. AUSTRALIANS.

The mental power of the Australians was first treated with the greatest contempt, but now we find that they possess a highly artificial language, and even boast of poetry and poets.

For thirty-six years these aborigines defied all endeavours to convert or even to civilise them. Various missionary societies made the attempt in vain. The darkness of doom gathered on them. But at length, in 1860, Nathaniel Pipper, a native of the colony of Victoria, became converted and was baptised, on which surprising event a public meeting was held to celebrate the occasion with thanksgiving, at which the Governor took the chair. This example has been followed, and now there are flourishing native Christian communities in several parts of the great territory.[2]

[1] *Pioneering in New Guinea*, p. 284.
[2] See *Australian Pictures*, pp. 176, 177.

A CIVILISED AUSTRALIAN LUBRA.

A CIVILISED AUSTRALIAN ABORIGINAL.

We read of old Norah, one of the squalid natives, having before her conversion the manners of an idiot and all the sins of a savage. Yet afterwards she became a bright, earnest, and faithful believer in Christ.[1]

10. SANDWICH ISLANDERS.

We proceed to the Sandwich Islands. One of the most robust characters in the history of these islands was Kanhumanu, the regent of the islands from 1823 to the time of her death in 1832. She was a woman of superb appearance and bearing, and of great energy, decision, and ability. She was distinguished by pride, haughtiness, and rigour, while yet a heathen; but about the year 1821 she came under the influence of the Gospel, and thenceforward became, though not less powerful and skilful as a ruler, a humble, devout Christian. In her religious acts and communications she ascribes the change to the recognition by her mind of the love and work of Christ. Her historian says: 'For one born and nurtured in heathenism, so long familiarised with its superstitions and abominations, with her disposition, and after a proud and absolute sovereignty of thirty years, the change was certainly remarkable.'

The grounds of this change may be inferred from the incidental language of a letter which she addressed to her friend the superintendent of the American Mission, dated Oahu, September 11th, 1831: 'This is my thought for you, and my joy. I now abide by the voice of the Saviour, Jesus Christ, who hath

---

[1] *Evangelical Alliance Conference*, 1873.

redeemed me from death. . . . When I heard the voice of Jesus as it sounded in my ear, it was refreshing to my bosom, saying thus, "Come unto Me, all ye that labour and are heavy laden, and I will give you rest;" and again, the voice of Him who said, "Whosoever is athirst, let him come and drink of the water of life." Therefore I arose and came. . . . Therefore do I bear His yoke. This one more thought to make known to you; make known my love to my brethren in Christ, and to my beloved sisters in Christ Jesus. This is my salutation to you. Pray ye all to God for all the lands of dark hearts.'[1]

II. POLYNESIANS AND MELANESIANS.

The Pacific Archipelago, as already stated, is divided into Polynesia, Melanesia, and Micronesia. The first lies between the Sandwich Islands and New Zealand; the second (dark people), is the name applied to New Guinea and its surroundings; the third, the region of the little islands, applies to a ring of islets extending from about 135° to 180° west longitude abutting on the equator. The people are light brown in colour and tall in stature, with thin noses and scanty beards. Those in whom the negro type prevails, the Papuans and inhabitants of the northern islands, are classed as Melanesians. Where the Malay type prevails they are styled Polynesians; but they are greatly mixed.

The morals and manners of the Polynesians before the introduction of Christianity were indescribably

[1] Anderson, *Sandwich Islands*, p. 104.

bad. The tales of the old voyagers, and the narratives of the early missionaries prove this. Their mythologies are highly fanciful. They had 'gods many,' for almost everything, animate or inanimate, was made the subject of a religious myth, and an object of some kind of worship. They were eminently religious in the sense in which the ancient Athenians were; they recognised every action with a kind of prayer, and made frequent offerings to their deities. Witchcraft and sorcery were universal beliefs, divination a regular profession.

Yet here also we are able to register some of the most notable instances of the correspondence between the needs of humanity and the provisions of revelation. Mr. Nott, a missionary in the South Sea Islands, having read on one occasion the third chapter of the Gospel by John to a number of the natives, some of them appeared deeply impressed. When he had finished the sixteenth verse, one of them, very much affected, interrupted him, asking, 'What words are those you read? What sounds were those I heard? Let me hear those words again.' Mr. Nott again read the verse, 'God so loved the world that He gave His only begotten Son.' The poor pagan then rose from his seat and said, 'Is that true? Can that be true? God love the world, when the world would not love Him! God so loved the world as to give His Son to die that man might not die! can that be true? Mr. Nott read the verse again, told him it was true, and that was the message God had sent to them, and that whosoever believeth in Him should not perish, but be happy after death. The overwhelming feelings of the wondering pagan were too powerful for expression or for restraint. At length he burst into tears, and as these rolled down his dark visage he withdrew to meditate in private on the amazing love of God which had that day touched his heart. There was every reason to believe that he was afterwards raised to share the joys of Divine peace, the fruits of the love of God shed abroad in his heart.

Long before the introduction of Christianity into the South Sea Islands, two of the commonest Rarotongan proverbs were, 'Oh, for a Divine brother, as Tapai was wont to say,' and 'Oh for a Divine protector.' This was a feeling after God, which, as Mr. William Gill says, 'represented the heart-weariness of thoughtful men with the old state of things.'[1] When the Earl of Pembroke visited Rarotonga large gifts of island produce were made to him. In presenting them Tearikitaraaere referred to the fact that the earl was a stranger, and that in the olden time strangers were put to death, adding these noble words, 'In Jesus Christ all the world are kin.'[2] Makea David, the King of Rarotonga, wrote to the missionary an account of the death of Makea, the late king, who had died during the absence of the missionary. He said, 'Makea died with faith in the blood of Jesus the Messiah.'

In Williams's *Missionary Researches in the South Sea Islands* we read that 'the converts to Christianity in Raiatea, one of the Society Islands, and the largest of the group, were many of them so intelligent, and so free and correct in their conversation and address, that the officers of an English vessel

---

[1] *Sunday at Home*, 1875, p. 683.
[2] *Jubilee Volume of the Religious Tract Society*, p. 515.

then in port were led to question their originality, and to assert that they were mere parrots, repeating only what Mr. Williams, the missionary, had taught them.' To test this point Mr. Williams proposed to the captain and chaplain of the vessel to take tea at his house, when he would have ten or fifteen of the native Christians present, and they might answer any questions that should be proposed to them. This was agreed to, and the meeting was accordingly held. The natives were subjected to a protracted examination, in which they acquitted themselves to the satisfaction and surprise of their sceptical interrogators. To a question on the divine origin and inspiration of the Bible several had replied in a thorough manner, and when it came to an old priest, then a devoted Christian, instead of replying at once, he held up his hands and rapidly moved the joints of his wrists and fingers, then opened and shut his mouth, and closed these singular actions by raising his leg and moving it in various directions. Having done this, he said, 'See, I have hinges all over me; if the thought grows in my heart that I wish to handle anything, the hinges in my hands enable me to do so; if I want to utter anything the hinges to my jaws enable me to say it; and if I desire to go anywhere here are hinges to my legs to enable me to walk. Now,' continued he, ' I perceive great wisdom in the adaptation of my body to the various wants of my mind; and when I look into the Bible and see there proofs of wisdom which correspond exactly with those which appear in my frame, I conclude the Maker of my body is the Author of that Book.'

After a trial of over three hours, the captain and

chaplain were convinced that the converts were not 'parrots,' but spoke from their own native force of mind and abundant knowledge of the Scriptures. On their return to England they made a report highly favourable to the mission and to the character of the converts.

'As a witness from Rarotonga, we may cite Taraaere, a converted native of good character and great intelligence, who, when referring to the very general custom among the Polynesians of placing in the grave the weapons or tools of the deceased, with portions of food, said by way of contrast and alluding to this custom: "The dying sinner needs the one offering on Calvary, and that only, in order to appear acceptably in the presence of God." This was the more impressive, as Taraaere had been a high priest of the heathen deities, was about ninety years of age, and had been accustomed to offer human sacrifices to the god of Rarotonga.'[1]

We may well sing:—

> 'Creation's works in all their forms,
> From rolling stars to creeping worms,
> In never-ceasing concord join
> To sing Thy name, Thy power divine.
>
> But when the dawn of heaven we view
> In ruined sinners formed anew;
> When, in the Gospel's brighter skies
> We see the Sun of glory rise,
>
> No more we ask the stars to tell
> What Jesus only could reveal;
> In Him at once our eyes behold
> More than creation ever told.'

---

[1] W. W. Gill in *The Sunday at Home*, 1882, p. 549.

Mr. William Gill, in his *Jottings from the Pacific*, gives an example of the fitness of Bible truth concerning sanctification to the needs of the soul. 'A young native, just converted, remarked at a prayer meeting: "I want to tell you my little thought. It is this: We are just like forest trees felled for a new church, crooked, twisted, branching this way and that, with innumerable blemishes. It is of no use to try to make ourselves better, but let us at once drag our hearts with all their faults and sins to the feet of Jesus. He will by His Holy Spirit so alter, trim, and change us, that eventually we shall be made pillars in the temple of God."'

The following speech was made by a native of Mangaia, one of the South Sea Islands. Addressing the Church members he said: 'Brethren'—and pausing a moment, he continued, 'Ah! that is a new name; we did not know the proper meaning of that word in our heathenism. It is the *evangelia à Jesu* that has taught us the true meaning of the word "brethren." But am I here—here in the midst of the Church of Jesus? What a marvel! I marvel, you marvel—I here! It is the boundless love of God—you all know me.' Pointing to a man about his own age, he continued: 'Do you not remember the man whom he killed on yonder hill, and whose body he cooked and ate?' He mentioned three others by name, whom he and others of the Church had thus devoured in cannibal feasts; and then, with tears running down his cheeks, he exclaimed: 'Oh, the love of God! how far beyond all measurement! These hands have killed eleven men during the reign of Satan here, and whose bodies, with those of many others, I have eaten in our feasts."[1]

The tablet erected in memory of Dr. John Geddie, missionary of the United Presbyterian Church of Nova Scotia, and the first who secured a footing in the New Hebrides, bears the following striking inscription: 'When he landed in 1848 there were no Christians here, and when he left in 1872 there were no heathens.'

Bishop Patteson, writing in the midst of his Melanesian islanders, recounting conversations with them, quotes from one of the questions put to him: We believe that God loves us, because He sent Jesus to become a man and die for us.'

In writing of the Hervey Islands, Mr. William Gill makes the following statement, which affords evidence for our present contention: 'In translating the Scriptures into the language of this people, and in expounding to them the Gospel of salvation by Jesus Christ, we have no need to introduce foreign words to represent ideas of God and sin, and atonement and salvation, but we adopt their own words, and express sentiments and feelings in accordance with the doctrine of Christianity, and which are in a measure understood and appreciated by those whom we seek to instruct and bless.'[2]

[1] *Presbyterian Foreign Mission*, 1857.
[2] *Gems from the Coral Islands*.

12. NEW ZEALANDERS.

In 1814 Mr. Marsden first landed in the Bay of Islands, purchased a plot of land from the chief, and began to instruct the natives, a powerful, intelligent

A MAORI CHIEF.

savage race, practising cannibalism, and steeped in the grossest superstition.

In 1842, such had become the success of the mission carried on by the Church of England, a bishop was appointed. He wrote thus :—

'We see here a whole nation of pagans converted to the faith. A few faithful men, by the power of the Spirit of God, have been the instruments of adding another Christian people to the family of God. Young men and maidens, old men and children, all with one heart and one voice praising God; all offering up daily their morning and evening prayers; all searching the Scriptures to find the way of eternal life; all valuing the Word of God above every other gift; all in a greater or less degree bringing forth and visibly displaying in their outward lives some fruits of the influence of the Spirit. Where will you find through the Christian world more signal manifestations of the presence of that Spirit, or more living evidences of the kingdom of Christ?'[1]

Mr. Yate, who was well acquainted with the country, gave the following facts at a meeting in London in 1835: 'When the Scriptures were first translated into the language of New Zealand they were received very eagerly by the whole of the people, and all were desirous by some means or other to obtain a copy. In consequence of our having formed elementary schools about 800 could read; and almost immediately after the Scriptures were brought into use the whole of those persons were supplied with them. They purchased them by their own industry. I have not given away a single copy; they were so desirous to obtain them that they were willing to work six weeks each for the few copies we could put into their hands; and they value them more, and take more care of them than if we had given them; as

---

[1] *From Pole to Pole*, pp. 363, 364.

A MONGOL LAMA.

they look upon them more as their own property when they have to work for them. When they receive copies they invariably take them home to their families, and read them morning, noon, and night. I have gone into native villages where a few years ago I should scarcely have been admitted, and I have seen half a dozen parties assembled reading the Scriptures, deliberating upon them, and asking pertinent questions.'[1]

13. MONGOLS AND MONGOLOIDS.

The characteristic features of these are, prominent cheek-bones, a tendency to oblique setting of the eyes, straight hair, and brown, or brown-yellow skin. They extend over the greater portion of Northern Europe and Asia, over Polynesia, and throughout America in its aboriginal population. We have already touched on some of them, but there are so many gradations that it is difficult to define and classify them. We begin with the Turks.

These comprise the Ottoman Turks, the present ruling race in Constantinople and Egypt, and various Turanian tribes occupying territory from Eastern Siberia to the west side of the Black Sea. The Tartars and Ottoman Turks are Mohammedans, while many of the wandering tribes of the north-west are still pagans. The Turks hold a place in history as arrested conquerors. The Saracen has ever been the thorn in the side of the Greek Church, and often a terror to Rome. Their career of victory was turned back

[1] *Bible Conquests*, p. 283.

in battle at Tours in A.D. 732; at Granada in 1492; and at Vienna in 1683.

Gengis Khan (Ischenglis Khan) in the thirteenth century consolidated under one rule the tribes between China and Poland, and governed one of the greatest territorial empires which the world ever saw. But this vast empire was of transitory duration, and was superseded by the Mongol States as we now see them from China to North India.

The motley population occupying the area which bears now the name of the Turkish Empire speak diverse languages. In most of them the Gospel has some triumphs to record. The Report of the British and Foreign Bible Society for 1885 gives a table illustrative of the ethnological varieties united under one government, the great differences of language, and the desire springing up amongst them all for the possession of the Word of God. The Scriptures were during the year circulated as follows:—

Language	No. of copies sold.
Arabic	827
Armenian, Modern and Ancient	1,266
Armeno-Turkish (Turkish in Armenian letters)	497
Ararat Armenian, Armenian-Kurdish, each 8	16
Albanian, Gheg.	19
,, Tosk	135
,, Tosk with Greek, including 33 N.T.	618
Bulgarian	5,634
Slavic, more than half being N.T.	8,232
Greek, Modern	13,329
,, Ancient	5,131
,, with English, French or German	73
Greco-Turkish	1,559
Hebrew	2,684
,, with French, German, Bulgarian, or Turkish	137

Language.	No. of copies sold.
Judæo-Spanish, &c., with or without Hebrew	400
Ruman	60
Russ	443
Servian	29
Croatian	13
Turkish in Arabic letters for Mohammedans	3,903

The American missionaries carry on a very large work of education and evangelisation in Turkey. They find the Mohammedan population to be very difficult of access, but there are instances of conversion, though few and far between, showing that through them the immovable Turk is touched by the Gospel.

There are in the Turkish Empire some 40,000 children in mission schools, where they are carefully instructed in religious truth. There are over 1,000 pupils in the colleges established now at five points in the empire, and there are as many more in higher educational institutions for girls, where they are being trained to be teachers and native assistants. The mission presses are printing millions of pages annually where a few years ago they were printing only thousands. The Bible work in Turkey is indeed a marvel, seven new translations of the Bible have been made in different languages within a generation of American missionaries, and there are twenty-one complete sets of electrotype plates now in Turkey for printing as many editions of the Bible in various languages. Not far from 2,000,000 copies of the Holy Book have been already circulated.

An extract from a letter written by Miss Laura Luckee of the American Mission at Adanas in the Turkish Empire to the Secretary of the Religious

Tract Society will serve to show what is the real factor in the missionary enterprise among the population of Asia Minor. She writes: 'Heretofore of any one to whom the Moslems and Fellahîn felt specially drawn, they have been in the habit of saying: "He is a good man, cursed be his religion!' Now the encomium is: "May the man and his book [the Bible] and his religion be blessed of God!" Enquiry about Christ has begun.'

14. LAPPS. FINNS. ESKIMOS.

The great Ural-Altaic family comprises the Finns and Lapps, with their northern congeners in Europe, and the vast Mongolian people occupying the north of Asia, from the Samoiedes on the east to the confines of Germany on the west. The Greenlanders and Eskimos are included in this range. The Samoiedes, inhabiting the country bordering on the Arctic Sea, are Northern Turanians, principally migratory and mostly pagan. They are ethnologically related to the Finns. The Lapps are Finns, and preserve the original wandering habits of the race. The religion of the pagan Greenlanders or Eskimos consists in a belief in the power of spirits for good or evil, and in witchcraft.

From memoirs of Thomas von Westen, the apostle of the Lapps, we extract a statement relating a second evangelistic visit to them. He says: 'Almost everywhere I found the Lapps who had received my testimony during my first visit steadfast in the good profession. The Holy Spirit had

LAPPS.

sustained them in all temptations from within and without for their own eternal benefit, and to the comfort and joy of the man who bore them on his heart day and night with a father's love. I noticed, to my great joy, that wherever the Lapp went he had his book in his bosom, God's Word on his lips, and Christ for his friend. In more than one miserable hovel the gospel of peace and salvation was received, and joy in the Lord took the place of resistance and perverseness of heart.' In one place the Lapps had determined on shooting Mr. Westen and his companions, but he had hardly arrived when their hatred was changed into the warmest affection and to the godly sorrow that worketh repentance.

The Finns exist at the very edge of the habitable globe, towards the north. They stretched down into Hungary as Magyars, and are supposed to have formed the principal Turanian population of Europe before the Celts appeared. There are several branches and varieties; some small and ill-conditioned as the Lapps, and others handsome and well proportioned as the Hungarians. Forty thousand tracts containing evangelical doctrine were published and supplied at the request and for the use of the Finns in the year 1885.

On January 19th, 1733, Christian David, with two of his cousins, left Moravia for the country of the Greenlanders, in order to introduce the Gospel to the forlorn heathen of that ice-bound country. Two of the natives had visited Copenhagen, and the sight of them moved the brethren to their apparently desperate undertaking of philanthropy. The spirit which animated them found expression in the simple verse by which they cheered each other—

> 'Lo, through ice and snow we press,
> One poor soul for Christ to gain,
> Glad we bear want and distress
> To set forth the Lamb once slain.'

They found the natives so ignorant and barbarous that they concluded it would be in vain to preach the Gospel to them, and they set themselves to teach them the nature and attributes of God, and the great truths of theism. Year after year they continued this teaching without the least effect.

In a letter sent to Germany about this time, they write as follows: 'How does it abase us, when we receive by the ship accounts of the success of our fellow-labourers among Christians and heathens, and especially of the abundant harvest now reaping in St. Thomas, while poor we must go away empty. But courage, dear brethren! Let us believe that the Lord will still do glorious things in Greenland. Do not intermit your supplications that God would display His power in the hearts of these poor people.'

Two days after this letter was sent off, the first Greenlander—a wild native of the south, quite unknown to them, and who had never heard a word about God—was awakened by the doctrine of Jesus's sufferings. We shall relate this important event as nearly as possible in the missionaries' own words:—

'*June 2nd.* Many of the natives of the south that passed our habitation visited us. John Beck was at the time just writing a translation of the Evangelists. The savages earnestly requested to hear the contents of that book. He accordingly read part of it, and took the opportunity to enter into some conversation with them. He asked them if they had an immortal soul? They answered, "Yes." He asked, again, where their souls would go after death? Some said, "Up yonder," pointing to the sky; others, "Down into the abyss." After setting them to rights, he asked them who had made heaven, earth, and everything visible? They replied that they did not know, nor had ever heard, but that it certainly must have been some great and opulent lord. He then told them how God had created all things good, particularly man, but that the latter revolted through disobedience, thereby plunging himself into extreme misery and ruin. But that the Creator had mercy on him, and became man to redeem him by suffering and dying. And now, said Brother Beck, we must believe in Him if we wish to be saved. The Holy Spirit then prompted this brother to give them an energetic description of the agonies of Jesus.

'He exhorted them to consider seriously how much it had cost our Saviour to purchase their redemption how He had been wounded, suffered inexpressible anguish, sweat blood, and died a cruel death for their sakes; and how awful would be their responsibility should they reject His offer of grace. He afterwards read to them from the New Testament the narrative of Christ's sufferings on the Mount of Olives. Then the Lord opened the heart of one of them called Kayarnak, who stepped up to the table and said with a loud, earnest, and affecting voice: "How was that? tell me once more, for I would fain be saved too." These words,' said the missionary, 'the like of which I had never heard from a Greenlander before, thrilled through my frame and melted my heart to such a degree that the tears ran down my cheeks, while I gave the Greenlanders a general account of our Saviour's life and death, and of the whole counsel of God concerning our salvation.

'Meanwhile the other brethren returned from their several employments, and began to explain the doctrines of the Gospel to the heathen still more at large. On the 18th of June a great number of the natives visited us again. Most of them were deaf to the Gospel. But it became more and more apparent that divine truth had made an indelible impression on the heart of Kayarnak. He is continually repeating either a short ejaculation or a text that he has heard from us, and is now come entirely to live with us. When we speak to him the tears frequently roll down his cheeks. His peculiar intelligence is surprising when compared with the supineness and stupidity of the other Greenlanders, who can scarcely comprehend what is duly repeated to them. But this man scarcely hears a truth before he understands it so as to retain it in his memory and heart. He is also exceedingly affectionate, and shows a constant desire to be instructed, catching every word with an eagerness which we have never observed in a Greenlander before. His family or tent companions were the first who were benefited by the conversation of Kayarnak; but before a month had elapsed three large families of South Greenlanders came and pitched their tents near the mission-house. They came to hear the joyful news of their redemption; and when the brethren could not find suitable expressions, the new convert helped them from the fulness of his heart.'

The Eskimo family brought into Germany in 1880 (all of whom speedily died from fever and decline) were native Christians. It was a striking sight to see and hear them, hand in hand, with their Teutonic brethren at Berlin, responding with joy to the name of Jesus, and singing together hymns to His praise. The short, beardless, broad-shouldered, flat-faced, small-eyed, brown, straight-haired people from the Arctic circle, in the same choir as the tall, fair-haired Germans, having little in common but faith in the grace of Christ.

15. THE AMERICAN ORIGINAL RACES.

These are for the most part termed red-men, but this appellation is only characteristic of a comparatively few tribes. The native population, whether wandering Indian tribes or semi-civilised inhabitants of Central America, or Patagonians and southern wild Indians, have some features in common. Professor Flower says: 'The mental characteristics of all the American tribes have much that is common; and the very different stages of culture to which they had attained at the time of the conquest, as that of the Incas and Aztecs, and the hunting and fishing tribes of the north and south, which have been quoted as evidence of diversities of race, were not greater than those between different nations of Europe, as Gauls and Germans on the one hand, and Greeks and Romans on the other, in the time of Julius Cæsar.'[1]

They belong to the yellow race, and share several of their characteristics, and there seems good reason to

---

[1] *Nature*, 1885, p. 365.

hold that they sprung originally from Asia. The primitive religion of these tribes was pagan, but of a high character.

The Mohawks worshipped the Great Spirit, as the good and beneficent giver of every blessing, and once a year dressed a *white* dog in bright colours, shed his blood, and burnt him as a sacrifice, believing that their prayer and grateful thanks for the good things of earth would ascend to the Great Spirit in the smoke.

Brainerd, in his journal amongst the Red Indians, after noticing how all his useful preaching was based on the doctrine of Christ crucified, says: "It was remarkable, when I was favoured with any special freedom in discoursing of the ability and willingness of Christ to save sinners, and the need they stood in of such a Saviour, there was then the greatest appearance of Divine power in awakening souls, promoting convictions begun, and comforting the distressed."

In 1734 the Moravian missionaries worked among the Indians of the Mohican tribes, and gained converts there. Ischoof gave the brethren the following simple, yet interesting, account of his conversion. 'I,' said he, 'have been a heathen, and have grown old among the heathen, therefore I know how the heathen think. Once a preacher came and began to tell us there was a God. We answered him saying: "Dost thou think us so ignorant as not to know that? Go back to the place whence thou camest!" Then another preacher came to us, and began to say, "You must not steal, nor lie, nor get drunk." To him we answered, "Thou fool, dost thou think that we do not know that? Learn first thyself, and then teach thine own people, and leave off these practices. For who steal or lie, or who are more drunken than the white men?" Thus we dismissed him. After some time, Brother Ranch came into my hut and sat down by me. He then spoke to me as follows, "I am come to you in the name of the Lord of heaven and earth. He sends to let you know that He will make you happy, and deliver you from that misery in which you at present lie. For this purpose He gave His life a ransom, and shed His blood for us." When he had finished his discourse, he lay down upon a board, fatigued by his journey, and fell into a sound sleep. I then thought, What kind of a man is this? There he sleeps. I might kill him, and throw him out into the wood, and who would regard it? But this gives him no care or concern. At the same time I could not forget his words. They constantly recurred to my mind. Even while I slept I dreamed of that blood which Christ shed for us. I found this to be something different from what I had ever heard before, and I interpreted Christian Henry's words to the other Indians.

'Thus, through the grace of God, an awakening began amongst us. Brethren, preach Christ our Saviour, and His sufferings and death, if you would have your words to gain entrance among the heathen.'

A Red Indian living in the wild reserves in North America recently came 600 miles to find a missionary in Minnesota, who thus tells the story: 'He came and knelt at my feet and said, "My fathers told me that there was a Great Spirit, and I have often gone to the woods and tried to ask Him for help, and I can only get the sound of my voice. One day an Indian came to my wigwam, and said that he had heard you tell a wonderful story at Red Lake, that you said the Great

Spirit's Son had come down to earth to save all the people that needed help. They told me you would be at the Red Lake crossing; I came 200 miles, I did not find you, as you were sick, but I went 150 miles more to find a missionary. I found that he was a red man ike myself. My father, I have been with him three moons—I have the story in my heart—it is no longer dark."'[1]

This is the old, old story without a doubt.

The Hydahs are a tribe of wild Indians, living in Queen Charlotte's Islands in Canada, in the far Northwest. They are idolaters, but have yielded in a measure to Gospel influence. That which has found its way to their hearts and consciences is the love of Christ in His expiatory death for sinners. As the old chief says, 'I lie awake and cry to God to pardon my own sins, and to save me. I know it is true, all true, and I want to be safe in the ark.'

In 1843 Paten Jacobs, an Indian of the Chippewa nation, felt convinced of sin under the preaching of a missionary, and relates that he went into a hayloft, and prayed to Christ for redemption, 'Now, O Jesus, the Saviour of the world, apply now Thy precious blood to my heart, that all my sins may depart! I was restless and could not sleep, I made another effort to pray to Christ, and before daybreak I found that my heavy heart was taken away and I felt happy. I felt the joy which is unspeakable and full of glory. Then I found that Jesus was sweet indeed to my soul. Then after that I had a desire that all my people should know the Saviour, and in my feeble way I have been

---

[1] *Illustrated Missionary News*, July 1878.

NORTH AMERICAN INDIAN.

endeavouring to do good ever since to the present time.'

Nicodemus was the name of an Indian convert under the Moravian missionaries in North America as early as 1742. He proved a very faithful Christian helper, and died in peace, saying, 'I am poor and needy, and therefore amazed at the love of my Lord Jesus Christ, who is always with me.'

Once when he was looking at a mill at Guadenhuten, he addressed a missionary thus: 'Brother, I discover something that rejoices my heart—I have seen the great wheel, and many little ones; every one was in motion and seemed all alive; but suddenly all stopped, and the mill was as dead. I then thought, "Surely all depends on one wheel; if the water runs upon that everything else is alive, but when that ceases to flow, all appears dead." Just so it is with my heart. It is a dead wheel. But as soon as Jesus' blood flows upon it, it gets life, and sets everything in motion, and the whole man being governed by it, it becomes evident that there is life throughout. But, when the heart is removed from the crucified Jesus, it dies gradually, and at length all life ceases.'[1]

> 'Nature through all her ample round
> Thy boundless power proclaims,
> And in melodious accent speaks
> The goodness of Thy names.
>
> Thy justice, holiness, and truth
> Our solemn awe excite,
> But the sweet charms of sovereign grace
> O'erwhelm us with delight.'

[1] *History of Moravian Missions*, p. 104.

'A missionary was once preaching to an Indian congregation, in the North-western territories, on the subject of Christ and Him crucified, describing the scene at Gethsemane, and pointing to the unbefriended Sufferer on the cross. The congregation was much affected, and soon a tall son of the forest with tears on his red cheeks, approached the pulpit and said, "Did Jesus die for me—die for poor Indian? Me have no lands to give to Jesus, the white man take them away. Me give Him my dog and my rifle." The minister told him Jesus could not accept those gifts. "Me give Him my dog, my rifle and my blanket, poor Indian, he got no more to give he give Jesus all." The minister replied that Jesus could not accept them. The poor ignorant child of the forest bent his head in sorrow and meditated. He raised his noble brow once more, and fixed his eye on the preacher, while he sobbed out: "*Here is poor Indian, will Jesus have him?*" The Spirit had done His work, and he who had been so poor sat at the feet of Jesus, heir to the treasury of heaven.'[1]

Some time ago a poor neglected orphan among the Modoc Indians was adopted, when very young, by a missionary's wife. Soon after she came she found a picture of the Crucifixion, and asked her schoolfellows to explain what it meant. They referred her to the teacher, who told her in very simple words the story of the cross. As she went on with the history tears streamed down the face of the little girl, who did not speak for a while. Then her first words were, 'She never meant to do bad any more.' Her heart was so touched with the love of the Saviour who died

[1] *Journal of Missions*, 1859.

for our sins that she resolved never to grieve Him, but desired to please Him perfectly. From this resolution she never wavered, but became her teacher's right-hand girl, always ready to do her bidding, and she exercised a most beneficial influence on her class.

Mr. Pascoe writes to the London Association for the Distribution of the Scriptures under date July 30th, 1885, as follows:—

'It will interest you to know that God has honoured His Word so much in our Indian village of Santa Cruz, containing 422 souls, that we have now 292 of them decided Protestants, so that two-thirds of the whole village have been converted by your free-gift Scriptures. Will not this grand result of Gospel seed-sowing in seven years among Mexican Indians give you joy? remembering that the very first seed sown among them was one of your Bibles, and that the Indian who received it is now a preacher and prayer-leader, and is at this moment engaged in scattering the seed in places where no other sower has been previously.'

Red Indians are the sole inhabitants of all Guiana except a narrow strip lying along the coast. They are of many tribes, which, however, may be distinguished into two groups, according as they are of Carib or non-Carib origin. The non-Carib tribes, the most important of which are the Warraus and Arawaks on the coast, and the Wapranas in the interior, are obviously the older inhabitants of the land. The Carib tribes, consisting of the Macoosis, Arekronas, Ackawois, and True Caribs, represent a number of later immigrations into the land.

The Fuegians would be selected as the typical

specimens of the degradation and degeneration of the human race. After repeated failures between 1844 and 1851 to found a Christian mission in Patagonia, and the death by starvation on the wretched shores of Fuegia of the gallant Captain Allen Gardiner in the last-mentioned year,—after the scientific world, headed by Darwin, who had visited them in the *Beagle*, had pronounced it impossible to introduce morality amongst them, the devoted friends of the Gospel persevered, and introduced the preaching and teaching of Christ and Him crucified. They laboured under the auspices of the South American Missionary Society, and their work has issued in the conversion of a considerable number of the natives, and in their transformation from horrid barbarism to honest and intelligent manhood. It is recorded as an established fact that the degraded Patagonians will respond to the appeal made to them by Christ on the cross. So true is His saying, 'I, if I be lifted up, will draw all men unto Me.'

Mr. B. Sulivan, in a letter to the *Daily News*, published April 29th, 1885, gives the full particulars of the late Mr. Darwin's ultimate and remarkable testimony concerning the Fuegians after they had received the Gospel:—

'Your article in the *Daily News* of yesterday induces me to give you a correct statement of the connection between the South American Missionary Society and Mr. Charles Darwin, my old friend and shipmate for five years. I had been closely connected with the society from the time of Captain Allen Gardiner's death, and Mr. Darwin had often expressed to me his conviction that it was utterly useless to send missionaries to such a set of savages as the Fuegians, probably the very lowest of the human race. I had always replied that I did not believe any human beings existed too low to comprehend the simple message of the Gospel of Christ. After many years —I think about 1869, but I cannot find the letter— he wrote to me that the recent accounts of the mission proved to him that he had been wrong and I right in our estimates of the native character, and the possibility of doing them good through missionaries; and he requested me to forward to the society an inclosed cheque for 5*l.* as a testimony of the interest he took in their good work. On January 30th, 1870, he wrote : "The success of the Tierra del Fuego Mission is most wonderful, and charms me, as I always prophesied utter failure. It is a grand success. I shall feel proud if your committee think fit to elect me an honorary member of your society." On June 6th, 1874, he wrote : "I am very glad to hear so good an account of the Fuegians, and it is wonderful." On June 10th, 1879 : "The progress of the Fuegians is wonderful, and had it not occurred, would have been to me quite incredible." On January 3rd, 1880 : "Your extracts" (from a journal) "about the Fuegians are extremely curious, and have interested me much. I have often said that the progress of Japan was the greatest wonder in the world ; but I declare that the progress of Fuegia is almost equally wonderful." On March 20th, 1881 : "The account of the Fuegians interested not only me, but all my family. It is truly wonderful what you have heard from Mr. Bridges about their honesty and their language. I certainly should have predicted that not all the missionaries in the world could have done what has been done." On December 1st, 1881, sending me his annual subscription to the orphanage at the mission station, he wrote: "Judging from the *Missionary Journal*, the mission in Tierra del Fuego seems going on quite wonderfully well." I have much pleasure in sending you these particulars.'

The Bible is translated and circulated in twenty-four versions among the North American Indians, and in ten versions amongst the natives of South America. From Labrador to Tierra del Fuego the glad tidings are being proclaimed.

AN EGYPTIAN FOOTMAN.

CHAPTER VII.

THE BROWN AND WHITE RACES ACCEPTING THE GOSPEL.

> 'What hath not man sought out and found,
> But his dear God? Who got His glorious law
> Embosoming in us, mellowing the ground
> With showers and frost, with love and awe;
> So that we need not say, Where's this command?
> Poor man! thou searchest round
> To find out *Death*, but missest *Life* at hand.'
> GEORGE HERBERT.

THE races included in this group are easily recognised, notwithstanding their remarkable divergence from the typical Aryan. In spite of their dissimilarity we have to place in the same ethnological class the Hindu, the Circassian, and the Serv. On examining their pedigrees they are all presumably traceable back to the highlands of Central Asia, the great central plateau fully described by Sir Richard Temple in his address at the British Association in the year 1882.[1] We use the word 'presumably' because absolute certainty in such researches is not attainable. Dr. Max

---

[1] *British Association Report*, 1882, p. 613.

Müller, in an article in *Good Words* for September 1887, containing a profusion of learning, says:—

'The question as to the original home of those who spoke Aryan, before the Aryans separated, will never admit of a positive answer, unless some quite unexpected evidence or some very ingenious combination shall be forthcoming. We must learn to bear with our horizons. It is wonderful enough that we should have discovered that our own language, that Greek and Latin, that Slavonic and Celtic are closely connected with the languages now spoken in Armenia, Persia, and India. It is wonderful enough that out of the words which all these languages, or at all events, some members of its two primitive branches, the North-Western and South-Eastern, share in common, we should have been able to construct a kind of mosaic picture of the fauna and flora of the original home of the Aryans, of their cattle, their agriculture, their food and drink, their family life, their ideas of right and wrong, their political organization, their arts, their religion, and their mythology. If an answer must be given as to the place where our Aryan ancestors dwelt before their separation, whether in large swarms of millions, or in a few scattered tents and huts, I should still say, as I said forty years ago, "Somewhere in Asia," and no more.'

I. HAMITES.

The Hamites comprise the Kopts of Egypt, the Nubians, and some kindred tribes. The modern Egyptians are a mixed race in which the original is the Berber. The natives are now called Fellahin when agricultural labourers, and when otherwise spoken of as Kopts. They are direct descendants of the ancient Egyptians, and they correspond in feature to the abundant representations in the tombs. The descendants of Ham are found in Nubia, Abyssinia and Algeria, as well as in Egypt.

The Hamites have demanded seven different versions of the Scriptures for the various dialects of North Africa, and are receiving them with interest and profit.

The United Presbyterian Mission of North America reported about 1863 that 'Weekly prayer meetings among the Kopts were started in four quarters of Cairo. One of these, which was held within a stone cast of the patriarchal palace, was changed into a *nightly* meeting for the study of the Scriptures, and was largely attended by intelligent young men belonging to the leading families of the Koptic community. They were drawn at first by curiosity, and were amazed to hear a Protestant praying for those who were cursing them.

'These young men became at length so interested in the object of the meeting that they resolved to open a similar one on their own account; to pray for themselves, as they expressed it, and invited all to assist them to organise and conduct it. This union meeting was held for a time in a hall of the patriarchal palace. A weekly prayer meeting was also commenced among the women, three of whom were ere long able to take part with the assistant teachers in conducting the devotional exercises.

'As evidencing the genuineness of the movement, all the twenty heads of families connected with the infant Church at Cairo formed themselves into a missionary society, pledging themselves at the same time to give to the Lord a proportion of their weekly income, according to their ability. Notwithstanding the poverty of most of the members, the sum for which they stood engaged for the support of one or more native evangelists amounted to £4 monthly.'

II. SEMITIC RACES.

The descendants of Shem form a well-known group with expressive countenances, thin lips, aquiline noses, curved eyebrows, oval faces, and more or less dark complexions. Hebrews, Canaanites, Assyrians, Babylonians, Armenians, and Arabs are readily distinguishable from other families of nations. In the modern world the Jew is present in nearly every commercial community. The Semitic nations were all originally monotheists, but long before the advent of Christianity many of them had become corrupted into polytheism.[1]

I. JEWS.

The districts pervaded by Semitic races in the ancient world were those between the Mediterranean and the mountains of Mesopotamia, Syria, Palestine, Phœnicia, Arabia, and Chaldea. As colonists they extended to spots along the Mediterranean as far as Carthage. They have always been the traders of the world; their language has been the chosen medium of Divine communication, and to one of their races according to the flesh belongs the infinite honour of the Divine incarnation.

The records of the Protestant Societies established

---

[1] See *The Early Prevalence of Monotheistic Beliefs*, by the Rev. George Rawlinson.—*Present Day Tracts*, vol. ii.

for Missions to the Jews abound in instances showing that the new light which the Israelites required in order to give them true peace was the light shed by the cross of Christ into the heart of the believer. The most recent publication on these Missions is the memoir of Dr. Aaron Stern, the well-known Abyssinian captive. A number of cases are brought together in this memoir which illustrate our argument. Of course the familiarity of the Hebrews with the doctrine of sacrifice affords an avenue for the entrance of the truth concerning the Great Sacrifice; and a scholarly Jew has quite recently published a small work in which he proves that Christianity is the only religion which reveals a plan of salvation in harmony with infinite wisdom and the cravings of the sinful heart.[1]

It is remarkable that the rules of a society formed by and amongst the Jews in England converted to Christianity lay down as a principle of their organization the following:—'Our bond of union is Jesus Christ, crucified and risen again, our Brother and our Divine Lord. As we have found in Him our personal Saviour, when He brought many—yea, all of us, by a way that we did not at first know whither it would lead—to the knowledge of the Gospel, so we believe that He will eventually bring all the lost sheep of the house of Israel, in a wonderful manner, to the fold, and will be the only Shepherd and Bishop of their souls.'[2]

The records of the recent mission to the Jews at Breslau publish the following case: 'Conspicuous above other encouraging tokens was the conversion,

---

[1] *Life of Stern*, by Isaacs. [2] *Life of Dr. Stern*, p. 471.

followed by the baptism on the first day of 1854, of Israel Pick. He had been school inspector and preached to the Jews in Bucharest, and by his philosophical attainments and oratorical powers had secured for himself a distinguished position.

'What had first arrested him was "the fact that all the progress which the world was now witnessing, scientific, moral, social, and political, was identified with Christianity. There must be something in it, thought he; it must have some mysterious vitality nowhere else to be found." On the occasion of his baptism he delivered before an audience of seven hundred persons, of whom several hundred were Jews, a lengthened address, which a not very friendly writer in a Breslau newspaper characterised as furnishing "evidence of rare rhetorical power."'

Already over three hundred students at the universities have joined the movement. It is stated in a German newspaper that in Vienna alone during 1885 two hundred and sixty Jews became Christians, and that never in the history of Germany were conversions from Judaism so numerous as now.

2. SYRIANS.

The population of Syria, roughly estimated, we learn from recent authentic information, is about 1,000,000, and a more complex, fragmentary, and mutually antagonistic people could not be found on the face of the earth. They comprise Moslems, Greek Catholics, Roman Catholics, Armenians, Maronites, Druses, Samaritans, Nusairiyeh, Ansairiyeh, Metawali, Jews, and Protestants. At least four of these—Druses,

Maronites, Samaritans, and Metawali—are not found elsewhere.

The American missionaries established a mission and set up a printing-press amongst them. The work of the latter has assumed proportions but faintly conceived of by those who founded it. As many as fifty *employés* are kept constantly at work, and are unable to supply the demands for printed truth that come from near and from far. Steam and hand presses are kept running from daylight until dark.

In 1885, 28,000,000 of pages were printed, and the number of volumes bound reached 881,000 ; 17,000,000 of these pages were Holy Scripture, and about 1,000,000 pages were tracts and sermons.

Amongst the motley population of Jerusalem itself it is most interesting to read such an account as the following from the records of the Church Missionary Society concerning the work of the Bible-woman supported by the Bible Society : 'When she first commenced work in Jerusalem she was treated very coldly and rudely, even by women who are accustomed to attend our services, and the Greek, Syrian, and Moslem women were indignant at the idea of any woman thinking that she could teach them anything, or presuming to urge them to purchase or to study carefully the Word of God. But now all is different. The Bible-woman is welcomed wherever she goes ; she is the most valued friend of her poor, ignorant, degraded sisters—hardly one of whom is able to read, and they delight to hear her read to them from the Bible of God's love and goodness, and of Jesus's wondrous work for their redemption.'

3. KURDS AND ARABIANS.

The Report of the Religious Tract Society for 1884 relates that 'one of our most valuable helpers among the Kurds has just died, and we are feeling his loss very deeply. His history shows how God by His providence and His Spirit, in ways all unknown to us, is bringing men to the knowledge and acceptance of the truth. Born of a Kurdish father and an Arab mother, his attention was first drawn to the Christian Scriptures by a fire-worshipper in Persia, who in some way become possessed of a copy of the Bible in Persian. The fact that Mohammed so often appealed to the Christian Scriptures for confirmation of his own doctrine struck the young inquirer as substantial proof of the superior authority of their Scriptures. After many wanderings to Bombay and other parts of India, ever seeking for truth, but, so far as appears, never coming, except in a most casual manner, into connection with missionaries, he arrived at length at Mosul on the Tigris. There he made the acquaintance of a most excellent Christian brother—a member of the Native Evangelical Church in Mosul, and was so impressed by the high character and blameless life of the man that he became thoroughly convinced of the superior claims of Christianity, and accepted it as the truth of God.'

[1] *Bithynia*, by Miss West.

ABYSSINIAN BOY.

The Bible is now translated and in demand all round the Caucasus in four dialects.

Well did Nathaniel Culverwell two centuries ago, write: 'Revealed truths are flaming darts of Heaven's shooting, that both open and enamour the soul. They are stars of Heaven's lighting; men behold them at a great distance twinkling in the dark. Whatsoever comes in God's name does either find or make a way.'

4. ABYSSINIANS.

The Abyssinians proper are the ancient Ethiopians. They are Semitic, and not Egyptian. They vary from black to coffee-colour, and appear to have characteristics both of the black and white races.

They are nominally Christian, but actually so superstitious and immoral that their religion is only a name.

5. BERBERS

The great Berber race, which has of late years given us so much concern in the Soudan, is the modern representative of the ancient Libyans. Amidst numerous waves of foreign invasion they have managed to hold possession of the vast territory lying between the Mediterranean and the equator, excluding the sea-board and Egypt.

The Berbers are a very ancient race, and still hold the northern coast of Africa. They form various tribes, and speak differing dialects of Arabic, and are now divided by the French colony of Algeria into Tripoli on the east, and Morocco on the west.

They are chiefly Mohammedan. They are usually classed with the Arabs as of Semitic descent, though many writers range them with the children of Ham. They are a rough, unamiable people, dark, and short in stature in the plains, but the mountain races are reported to be fairer and better looking.

Missionary attention is now being directed to them, and there is a special mission to the Kabyles and other Berber races. This encounters similar difficulties to other attempts among Mohammedans, but they are being approached by the soldiers of the Cross all along the line. The historic and long extinct Churches of North Africa—the arena of the great bishops before the Ottoman conquest, all seem to encourage the conviction 'that the truth as it is in Jesus' will again conquer this motley and bigoted people.

The Kabyles are principally Mohammedans; several of them have yielded to the influence of the love of Christ, as displayed in the Gospel preached by the missionaries of the North African Society.

Mr. Chusomen, one of the missionaries, says in his journal: 'Some Arabs came and read part of St. Matthew's Gospel, and the text on the walls, 'God so loved the world,' so fastened itself on the mind of one that when showing me his handwriting he wrote those words.'

A SYRIAN PATRIARCH.

I.

6. NESTORIAN SYRIANS.

The people now inhabiting the moorlands of North-west Persia are a branch of the great Semitic family. They are Arameans, and have a Syriac dialect similar to that which prevailed in Palestine in the days of our Lord. They are a pastoral people, and rarely till the soil. In religion they are unquestionably an off-shoot of Christianity. They were early converts, but retained much of Judaism, and separated from the Church in the fifth century, since which they have subsisted as a sect, but have never become a nation.

Mr. Pearce, an American missionary at Erzeroum, on one of his tours found his way to an almost inaccessible village on the mountain-top. He received a cordial welcome, and wrote 'that no missionary preacher or teacher had ever visited them, but they had a Bible and a hymn book, and the Holy Spirit was their teacher.'

Mrs. Mott writes from Beyrout, under date, March, 1885, concerning a mariner of Tyre: 'Some time ago Mr. Mott spoke to a seaman of the way of salvation as revealed to us in the Bible. The man could not read, but begged for a copy that he might get some friends to read it to him. Mr. Mott, however, impressed upon him the importance of learning to read, and search the Scriptures for himself. The man promised to do this, and gratefully accepted the book, and at once began to learn. Soon he felt much interest in its precious truths, and whenever he was able attended the simple services at Tyre. There the Lord met him, and he found the pearl of great price.

And now this simple Tyrian seaman is engaged among the sailors of Tyre, earnestly striving to bring them to the Saviour who has become so precious to his own soul.'

The Americans began a mission to the Nestorian Syrians in 1834, and after losses, sacrifices, and discouragement for some years, succeeded in bringing the message of the Gospel to the attention of the people, when it slowly but surely won its conquering way, not in wholesale conversion, but in unexpected cases here and there, 'one of a family or two of a city.'

The case of Deacon Ginvergis, a mountain evangelist, who previous to his conversion was as wild as any Kurd, was among the most remarkable outcomes of the revivals. Having in 1845 placed his daughter under Miss Fiske's care, he returned in the following year, with his belt of ammunition, his dagger at his side, and his gun thrown over his shoulder, to take her home. He found his daughter with others, weeping over her sins. He ridiculed her anxiety, but she urged him to go alone with her to pray. He went, and heard earnest prayer offered, first for herself, and then for her father. While she pleaded, 'Save, oh, save my father from going down to destruction!' he raised his hand to strike her, as he afterwards confessed. Sabbath morning found him still stoutly opposing this new influence, but he soon after broke down under Miss Fiske's affectionate appeals. He made his way to the church, leaving behind him his gun and dagger. In the evening he was found in the missionary's study, crying out in agony, ' My sins, my sins, they are higher than the mountains of

7. ARMENIANS.

The Armenians belong to the Aryan family; they are well made, dark, handsome people, and trusted and employed as honest, frugal, and industrious. They were magicians, worshippers of the elements, and especially worshippers of fire. Altars on which fire was kept continually burning were tended by priests who offered burnt sacrifices and propitiatory offerings as well to the element of fire as to rivers and lakes. Thence grew the religion of the Parsees, mingled with the precepts and creed of Zoroaster. Their sacred book is the Zendavesta.

Until quite recently the three millions of Armenians living within the Turkish empire, though not without God, were without any practical knowledge of Christ. About fifty years ago the doctrine of the Atonement was absolutely unknown among them, and their Christianity was purely nominal. At present the Scriptures in the vernacular are spreading both among the Western Armenians in Asia Minor and Turkey, and the Easterns in the Caucasus, Ararat, and Russia.

The diffusion of the Scriptures by the efforts of the American missionaries has led to this result. Dr. Dwight, in his *Christianity Revived in the East*, among other instances records the case of an

AN ARMENIAN FAMILY.

Armenian whose efforts to pacify an awakened conscience remind us of the pilgrimages and self-inflicted tortures with which Hinduism has made us familiar. From a convent which he entered in order to perform the most menial services for the monks, 'he penetrated into the depths of a wilderness, clothed himself in sackcloth, and lived on the coarsest fare.' Finding no rest to his soul, he returned to Constantinople, and having connected himself with the Romanists, hoped to secure the longed-for peace by a strict observance of the ceremonies of their Church.

But he was as far off as ever. At length he found his way with some friends to Mr. Hamlin's house. Taking a seat as near the door as possible, he listened in silence, then proposed some objections, but gradually became interested, and drew his chair nearer and nearer to his newly found teacher. At length he seated himself on the floor, literally at the feet of Mr. Hamlin, and then drank in with mute astonishment those Divine truths which he had never heard before, but which revealed to him the only sure foundation for peace of mind. There was an instantaneous change. 'He afterwards became a living witness of the truth, and a faithful labourer in the Kingdom of Jesus Christ.'

Pastor Catujian, a well-known Evangelical minister amongst the Armenians at Constantinople, thus writes: 'I can speak from my own experience and convince you, that during the ten years that this awakening has been going on, many have been deeply touched by the grace of the King of kings; and with this is united the earnest wish to become more and more partakers in the love and the prayers of all believers, of all who are brethren in the same Saviour.'

A few years ago, Miss West, a well-known American missionary, became very intimate with Aroosiag, an Armenian lady, one of the converts to evangelical religion. Aroosiag, in narrating to Miss West the history of her conversion, says : 'I saw that I was a sinner, and was much distressed for a long time. But one day while reading the hymn " I saw one hanging on a tree," Christ was revealed to me as my Saviour. Oh, Varzhooli [Miss West] I can never forget that verse :—

> 'A second look He gave that said,
> I freely all forgive ;
> This blood is for thy ransom paid,
> I die that thou mayest live.'

'What joy filled my heart! new life sprang up in my soul, and since then I am His and He is mine, and I have gone on my way rejoicing.'[1]

Although the Apostle Paul relinquished his wish to go into Bithynia, yet this was not on account of any want of adaptation in the race to the provision of the Gospel, as the result of the flourishing modern American mission among them testifies.

8. PERSIANS.

The staple population of Persia, the inhabitants of all the cities and fertile plains, are Aryans ; but the mountains are peopled by races of Turanian origin The Persians are Aryan Persians, so are the Afghans

---

[1] Miss West's *Bithynia*, p. 96.

but other hill races on the slopes and spurs of the Himalayas are Turanians, though resembling the Semitic Jews.

The Persian Zoroastrians and the Parsees of India are votaries of the shallow religion of Zoroaster, a religion of ritual and tabulated morals, but fatally wanting in adequate motive or sanction, and entirely wanting also in that which the universal conscience seeks—a sense of the Divine forgiveness of sin, a new life, and salvation. The Persians are a handsome dark race, with oval countenances, full dark eyes, and regular features. They extend into Armenia, Turkistan, and Afghanistan.

A few years after the death of Henry Martyn a traveller arrived at Shiraz, and was invited to dine at the house of a respectable native. Among the guests he noticed one, Mahomed Baber, who was more serious than the rest, and who expressed his surprise that the Christian foreigner did not show his disapprobation when the subject of religion was treated with levity. This circumstance impressed the stranger's mind, and he sought an interview with the Persian, who related the following narrative:

'A few years ago there came to this city an Englishman who taught the religion of Christ with a boldness hitherto unparalleled in Persia, in the midst of much scorn and ill-treatment from our moolahs as well as the rabble. He was a beardless youth, and evidently enfeebled by disease.

'He dwelt among us for more than a year. I was then a decided enemy to infidels—as the Christians are termed by the followers of Mohammed—and I visited this teacher of the despised sect with the

A PERSIAN LADY.

disclosed object of treating him with scorn and exposing his doctrines to contempt. Although I persevered for some time in this behaviour towards him, I found that every interview not only increased my respect for the individual, but diminished my confidence in the faith in which I had been educated. I gradually inclined to listen to his arguments, to inquire dispassionately into the subject of them, and finally to read a tract which he had written in reply to a defence of Islamism by our chief moolahs. Need I detain you longer? The result of my examination was a conviction that the young disputant was right. Shame, or rather fear, withheld me from avowing this opinion. I even avoided the society of the Christian teacher though he remained in the city so long. Just before he quitted us I could not refrain from paying him a farewell visit. Our conversation (the memory of it will never fade from the tablet of my mind) sealed my conversion. He gave me a book; it has ever been my constant companion; the study of it has formed my most delightful occupation; its contents have often consoled me."

Upon this he put into the stranger's hands a copy of the New Testament in Persian. On one of the blank leaves was written:—

'There is joy in heaven over one sinner that repenteth.—HENRY MARTYN.'

In 1823 an educated Persian youth, Menza Mahomed Ali Bey, who had been a violent opponent of Christianity at Astrachan, where he had come to reside, sought instruction from the Scottish missionaries there, and after some time, and the encounter of much persecution, embraced and confessed Christianity, avowing principles which we quote in support of the proposition we are endeavouring to prove. On the occasion of his baptism he said: 'When the Most High God of His boundless mercy presented to me the tidings of the Gospel, I read and saw that it gave information concerning a Saviour whom God Most High had made a propitiation for His sinful servant. I next reflected on my own sinful actions which I had committed in times past. I saw myself to be a sinner, and perceived what an enemy to God sin must be. In myself I had no hope of life whatever, nor of salvation from the wrath of God. . . . And after some days, in an hour of hours, my heart and soul and my whole frame gave me testimony that the blood of Christ has become a propitiation for all thy sins. If thou shouldest at this time die thou hast no cause to fear. To the praise of God from that hour to this my belief is, that Jesus Christ is the only begotten Son of God.—That His blood was shed for the sake of sinners,—and that, except the holy books above mentioned, there is no oracle from God."[1]

From the *Church Missionary Gleaner*, 1886, we extract the following instance, which is also in the exact line of our argument :—

'While at Oroomiah,' says the Bible colporteur, 'we went to visit Agha Syed Mirza Khaleel, the learned and intelligent dervish who has accepted Jesus Christ as his Lord and Saviour. He was a dervish (as his father was before him), and a respectable and clever one too. Some years ago he was led by the Holy Spirit to think of the sinful nature of

---

Christian Keepsake, 1856, p. 163.

man, and his need of a Saviour to save him from his sins, and thereby to make him fit for the kingdom of heaven. His soul, so to say, craved for his salvation; and according to his story the religion of Mohammed could not satisfy those cravings. Consequently, he became indifferent to that religion, and sought in other religions a salvation which might satisfy the longings of his soul. He left his village and travelled in Azerbijan, going about from place to place. He tried Baabiism and other branches of the Mohammedan religion in Persia, and Judaism, but all to no purpose. Being unsuccessful, he was obliged to return to his own place with a very heavy heart.

'He one day went to visit a friend. His eye happened to fall on a shelf, where a few books lay covered with dust. Being a learned man and a scholar, he got up to see what the books were, and the first which he took up was entitled the *Enjil* [New Testament]. He asked his friend what book it was, who told him that some time ago an Armenian goldsmith had presented him with it; but that, having read parts of it, he had found it to be a useless book, containing many queer things said of the prophet Jesus. On hearing this, he was moved with a desire to read the book; and opening it and reading a portion, he concluded that it could not be useless and queer as described to be. So he asked his friend to lend it to him for a few days, which he was not only glad to do, but presented the book to him. Taking it home, he began to read it from the beginning, and by the time he had finished it, he was, by the grace of the Holy Spirit, convinced of its truth.'

9. HINDUS.

The earliest known occupants of the world, excepting the Semitic races, were Turanians, who went forth and gradually peopled the river banks and coasts without making much progress in civilisation. The Aryans poured forth subsequently, probably, as we have seen, from Central Asia, in tribes which conquered or overbore by superior arts the previous population, and in process of time became the nationalities which we recognise as Hindus, Persians, Kelts, Teutons, Pelasgians, Phrygians, and Slavs.

The widest spread of this great family took place in the plains of India, where they still subsist in immense numbers, under English rule, principally known as Hindus, but comprising many nations and tribes bearing other appellations grounded on locality. The Hindu is a typical Aryan; the various hill tribes which he overran, and whose remnants are dotted over the whole peninsula, are Turanians, *i.e.*, Mongols.

The religion of the Hindu is a most extensive polytheism.

'The *Rig-Veda*, which embodies the early religious conceptions of the Indo-Aryan race, and which carries us back to a period of from 1000 to at least 1500 B.C., is a collection of hymns, invocations, songs of praise, addressed to various individuals or divinities—Indra Matia, Vayuna, &c., who seem at first sight to be personifications or deifications of the phenomena and forces of nature.'[1]

We now proceed to quote sundry instances of acceptance of the Gospel by individuals of the Hindu race.

[1] Dr. Macgregor's *Faiths of the World*.

NORTH INDIA.

A Hindu in Northern India who had heard a catechist, and become somewhat impressed, was put under religious instruction. When the catechist read to him and explained the Saviour's sufferings and death, he expressed great surprise, and said: 'Oh sir, is all this true? Is it true that He died for me?' The catechist replied: 'It is true.' Then said he: 'I have great joy in my heart; this is a great salvation.'[1]

How the converted Hindus esteem the peculiar doctrines of Christianity is shown by the report of the Rev. J. D. Bate, an experienced missionary at Allahabad. He says:—' The Trinity, the Atonement, the Deity of our Lord, the Personality of the Spirit, the Inspiration and Infallibility of Scripture, in a word the doctrine of "Christ crucified"—many a poor, despised native Christian would rather yield up his life than yield up his grasp of these.'

Mr. Wade, in charge of the Church Missionary Station at Amritsir, writes: 'Never before have I heard of a greater spirit of inquiry abroad, more intelligent and earnest religious discussions, more persons studying God's Word, some of them I know men of position and influence, and some truly hungering and thirsting for the bread and water of life. People from the district petition us to open mission-schools in their villages. I receive letters begging for books; numbers say privately they believe in Christ.'[2]

In the early days of the Baptist Mission in Bengal, Mr. Ward described the conversion of Rughoo, a

---

[1] *Wesleyan Missionary Herald*, March, 1858.
[2] *Report* for 1886, p. 102.

A NATIVE OF NORTH INDIA.

Hindu somewhat advanced in life, who had been the devoted slave of the priests. At six different times, according to the number of scars on his back, he had been swung in the air for a quarter of an hour each time suspended by large hooks thrust through the integuments of his back. Mr. Ward says: 'In one of my visits to him just before his death, I asked him some questions with reference to the presence of Christ with him, when he put his hand upon his heart and said: "He is here; I feel that He is here."'[1]

Another page may be taken from the early annals of the Bengal Mission:—

'A number of years ago, after preaching in the market-place, I left a New Testament at Ramkushnapur. From the perusal of this book is to be traced the conversion of Seterkram of Krishurdas, now an excellent and successful preacher, and of one or two other well-known Christian men.'

At Gorruckpur was a Mussulman of rank and influence, who received at baptism the name of Cornelius, though he is best known by his original name of Sheik Razud o Din. The Sheik was well educated, and much devoted to his religion. Hearing that his nephew was about to be baptised, he came to Gorruckpur determined to use forcible means to prevent his forsaking his own creed. To the entreaties of the youth that he would read the New Testament, and not condemn opinions which he had not examined, he turned a deaf ear; but when the missionary explained to him the peculiarities of the Gospel system, its suitableness to the case of fallen sinners, and its power to convey peace and happiness to the mind, he began to

Ward's *Letters*, 1822.

listen with more deference, and at last consented to accept a New Testament. About three months afterwards he returned to Mr. Wilkinson, and putting it into his hands, said that he had 'read it through and through.' The heart of that pious missionary glowed with thankful joy on hearing him add: 'When I received this book my heart was full of enmity to Christ as the Son of God, and I came here determined to pluck a lamb out of His arms. But this Saviour was too strong and too gentle for me. I am not only willing for my nephew to embrace Christianity, but I am now come to give *myself* to Christ, and to devote myself henceforth to His service.' From that time Sheik Razud o Din became a true and zealous follower of Jesus. On his dying bed his son held the Koran over him, and begged him to touch it. He pointed towards heaven, shook his hand as if to say, 'No, no; Christ is mine, and I shall be His for ever.'[1]

Mohesh Chunder Ghose, on his baptism, gave the following affecting account of his conversion:—

'A year since I was an Atheist, afterwards I turned to Materialism; I was unhappy beyond measure. And what am I now? A Christian, baptised in the name of Jesus, and indescribably happy. The retrospect of the past fills my mind with astonishment. I settled down in my philosophical principles, firmly resolved not to yield a step. I *hated* the Christian religion, and could not bear the thought of the possibility of being convinced of its truth. Yet I could not remain quiet. Against all my strongest resolutions, and contrary to the inclinations of my own heart, I was led step by step nearer to Christianity. I could not resist its evidences.

[1] *Missionary Sketches in North India*, pp. 348, 353.

When I heard your description of the nature of sin, especially of the sins of the heart, my conscience broke out like a volcano, my soul was racked, overcome by anxiety and terror. When I thought of some passages of the Bible I found a little more comfort. The doctrine of the Scriptures which appeared to me before pure nonsense, I now found to be divine wisdom What I formerly hated from my heart was now clear above everything. How shall I account for this change of mind? Impossible by natural principles. Everything went against my wishes, my preconceived resolutions; in opposition to all these I became a Christian! Surely an invisible power has conducted me hither. Something of what the Bible calls free grace must have exercised its influence upon me; and if ever a sinner has been converted by free grace it is I.'

Thus did a philosophical Hindu describe his conversion to Christianity.[1]

Miss C. Hanbury, of the Punjaub Village Mission, writes of the progress of Christianity among the coolie class in Northern India:—' A religious teacher from among this low caste people has for some time been interested in the teaching of the missionaries and more than once asked for a Gospel. When he at last got it, he read Matthew through at a sitting, he was so perfectly delighted. He said: " I have been seeking salvation, and could find it nowhere, but here it is."'[2]

About the year 1840 a Brahman went on a pilgrimage to Hurdwar, and there, at the most renowned *mela* in Hindustan, amid the din and throng of hundreds

---

[1] *Missionary Sketches in North India*, p. 60.
[2] *Life of Faith*, Aug. 1887.

INDIAN SNAKE CHARMER.

and thousands of devotees to the grossest idolatry, he received from a missionary some Christian books. He took them home with him, kept them for some years, but at length read them, and learned through them the truths of the gospel of salvation, which he communicated to his neighbours as he received them himself.[1]

CENTRAL INDIA.

The Rev. C. W. Park of the American Marathi Mission, at the Annual Meeting of the Religious Tract Society in 1881, gave the following narrative :—

'About 250 or 300 miles inland from Bombay, in the very centre of Hindostan, and perhaps in its darkest portion, the dominions of the Nizam of Hyderabad, is a little village. It is not on the line of any railway, nor approached by any great travelled road, but he who would reach it must go through lands and by-paths, over ploughed fields and waving corn, perhaps over the sterile and dusty plains of Central India. When he gets there he finds a little village with mud houses and around it a mud wall. That little village with its two or three hundred of people has a hereditary watchman, whose business it is to guard it day and night. He is now an old man, sixty years of age perhaps; his hair is grey, but in his earlier days he was known as a mighty man of valour, and worse than that, as a daring robber and leader of a gang of thieves, and for his excesses and crimes was apprehended and served

[1] *Missionary Sketches in North India*, p. 370.

a term in gaol. He returned to his village, and his conscience troubled him, and the feeling took possession of him, "I am a sinner; I have deserved evil, not alone of my fellow-men, but of my God;" and after the manner of his people he went from place to place, from one temple to another, from shrine to shrine, making his offerings, falling at the feet of his heathen gods, and striving to find peace to his troubled conscience. But there was no peace, his mind had no rest, and he knew not where to turn. I think it was in the year 1873 or 1874, that one day there came to his door a traveller, a Hindu like himself, a man of the lowest caste, who asked for water, and the old watchman brought forth the water and gave him, and then his visitor began to speak to him of a better water than this—of the living water, and told him where the soul burdened with a sense of sin might find rest, and peace, and joy. The watchman's soul was in just that condition that these words of life were indeed like water to the thirsty one, and his mind drank them in; and as he heard the words of everlasting life and salvation and of faith in the Lord Jesus Christ, he said, "This is the Saviour that I want, and here at the feet of Christ my soul finds peace."[1]

In the remarkable confession of Narayan Sheshadra, a Brahmin, who attended the Evangelical Conference held at New York in 1873, he says: 'There was one missionary to whom I am under special obligations, as it was he who made me thoroughly acquainted with the doctrines of justification by faith in Christ, and sanctification through the Spirit. The doctrine of the

[1] *Report of the Religious Tract Society*, 1882.

cross presented a sublimity to my mind that nothing else could equal.'

The Annual Report of the Church Missionary Society for 1886 relates the steps by which a young man, member of a rigid Buddhist family, was led to the Gospel. It says: 'When it was known that he had become a Christian, his father came to see him, to endeavour to win him back to Buddhism, but all his entreaties and promises were in vain. He said to his father: "I cannot go back to Buddhism; I must believe that there is a Creator of the world. I want forgiveness of sins, and there is no Saviour, no forgiveness, in Buddhism. I want to be happy after death, and there is no hope in Buddhism. I find all these in Christianity."'[1]

The Rev. E. P. Heberlet writes:—

'Once I went by express invitation to a silversmith's shop to compare our Scriptures with the Hindu Shastras. After I had read and spoken, the man and his friends declared themselves to this effect: "All the admirable points of your Scriptures can be matched by the excellences of ours, except this one of Christ dying for His *enemies*—for the wicked."'

The Zenana Missions have produced numberless proofs that the women of India, though deprived of society and learning, yet recognise the adaptation of the peculiar doctrines of Christianity to their deepest wants and highest aspirations. One of the lady missionaries, Mrs. Summers, writes of their festival of Juggernath in 1885:—

'On the last day of the festival, the day when

[1] *Report*, 1886, p. 164.

A HINDU WOMAN.

Juggernath was to be drawn back to his temple, the crowds were immense and the excitement very great. I accompanied Mrs. Ellis to the preaching station of the Zenana Mission, and we were there till evening speaking to the women. It was interesting to watch their faces while they were listening. Some were deeply interested and listened eagerly, others seemed amused to think we were trying to convince them of the uselessness of their religion, others were utterly indifferent and talked loudly to each other, and looked down the road. Two faces in that crowd stand out clearly in my memory. One was the face of a young woman eagerly listening, as though she could not afford to lose one single word of what was being said. I watched the eyes slowly fill and then overflow with tears, as she heard about Christ's love to men; but Christ as the "Man of sorrows and acquainted with grief" seemed to touch her most. At another time I was endeavouring to make her understand the doctrine of substitution, and speaking of Christ as having paid our debt. Her face beamed with intelligence, and she said, "Jesus has indeed done well for us." Thus every new lesson gave her new light, and she walked in it.'

Miss Joseph, in detailing the difficulties of a Brahman woman named Parvate, writes: 'The chronicles of the mission abound in instances of the acute sympathy of heart and mind with the doctrine of the great atonement.'[1]

When Taliboodeen, a highly intelligent Mohammedan soldier in the Madras army, who had become a Christian and suffered much loss and persecution on

[1] *Our Indian Sisters*, April, 1866.

this account, was asked what part of the Gospel narrative led him to decision, he replied with much tenderness, 'It was the story of the cross that broke my heart and for ever took my pride away. The story of Him who gave Himself to such a death so completely overwhelmed me that I sat down and wept three days.'[1]

SOUTHERN INDIA.

Southern India and Ceylon are partly occupied by descendants of the non-Aryan races, Tamils, Telugus, and others of whom we have before spoken; but, on account of their geographical connection with the Hindu populations, we have not attempted to separate these races in the following series of examples.

The Gospel was first preached at Travancore by a native gentleman, who had left it as a heathen, going on a distant heathen pilgrimage, in the course of which he went to Tanjore, and entered a place where a missionary was preaching Christ. The missionary, perceiving from his costume that he was a religious pilgrim, was more than usually in earnest in his appeal, and preached Christ, and uttered repeatedly the exhortation, 'Come to Jesus.' The pilgrim received the truth, and afterwards did all that he could do to diffuse the knowledge of the Divine Saviour.

The following decisive instance is from a recent book on South India.[2]

[1] *Sunday at Home*, 1877, p. 165.
[2] *The Gospel in South India; or, The Religious Life, Experiences, and Character of the Hindu Christians*, by the Rev. Samuel Mateer, of the London Missionary Society.

A HINDU BEARER.

'It is my impression,' writes Mr. Hacker, 'that many of the most thoughtful of the educated natives go secretly to Christ in the hour of sorrow, and lean upon Him in the hour of death. I experienced this year a striking illustration of this last statement which gave me much courage. Dr. Thomson was called to visit an old man belonging to a high caste, and to his surprise the man asked him if he could be baptised. The doctor came and told me about this, and I said, "By all means let him be baptised if he believes on the Saviour." The next morning, early, Dr. Thomson and I went to the house of this man. He was about seventy years of age, and would evidently soon pass from this world. I asked him if he loved Jesus, and if he was trusting Him for his soul's salvation. The old man said, "I am clinging humbly to His feet." It was worth coming to India to see this dying man's peace in the love of his Saviour. The remarkable thing is that he had never been in a Christian church, but years ago he bought a Bible, had been reading it privately, and its truth had fallen into his heart and brought forth this seed in his dying hour.'

The records of the American Mission furnish the following testimony from Southern India :—

'Nearly seventeen years ago a *gosari*, or religious mendicant, named Mhasoba, was sent to prison by the well-known Meadows Taylor for cattle stealing. While in prison he happily learnt to read. He had a friend, another *gosari*, who, after Mhasoba's release, came to him, telling him he had heard of some new and strange doctrines taught by white missionaries, and he wanted to find out what these doctrines were. "You now can read," he said ; "you can help me to

A NATIVE HINDU PASTOR.

find out what it all means." The two men consulted together, and decided that they would go and seek for the missionaries, who they heard were to be found at Sholapore. After a weary tramp of many days, to Sholapore they came. The missionary who was labouring then at this station was Mr. Harzen, Mrs Gates's father, who has now returned to America. He received the wayfarers most kindly, hearing their request, so similar to that of the Greeks to Philip : " We would see Jesus." He instructed them, gave them tracts and books, one of which was called the " True Way," and pointed them to Him who *is* the " Way, the Truth, and the Life." They carried the books back to their village, where Mhasoba read them aloud to his fellow-inquirers and the rest of the people. After much thought, and study, and earnest prayer, seeking the Lord with sincere hearts, " if haply they might feel after Him and find Him," they did find Him, as every real seeker does, and made up their minds that they would enter on this new way and become Christians.'

It is reported of a certain Hindu on the Malabar coast that he had inquired of various devotees and priests how he might make atonement for his sins, and find peace for his soul. At last he was directed to drive iron spikes, sufficiently blunt, through his sandals, and on these spikes he was to walk on pilgrimage to a celebrated heathen shrine, a distance of about 480 miles. He undertook the journey, and proceeded for some distance in much distress of both body and mind. Whilst sitting under a shady tree where the Gospel was sometimes preached, a missionary came and delivered an impressive sermon in the native language of the people, from the important text, 'The blood of Jesus Christ His Son cleanseth us from all sin!' The man believed the good news, and before the missionary had finished his discourse, he rose up, threw off his torturing sandals, and cried aloud, 'That is what I want!' and he became a living witness that the blood of Christ does indeed cleanse from all sin. By his subsequent life, and his humble, earnest efforts to bless others, he proved himself to be a sincere convert to the faith of the Gospel.[1]

The total number of Native Christians in all India, including Burmah, was returned, in the year 1881, as 528,598. The number of distinct versions of Scripture published for their use is about 33. It is estimated that there were 492,882 Protestant Native Christians in all India in the year 1881. As there has never been any government or public aid given to Christianity there,—and it has had to make its way against enormous social disadvantages—it may be affirmed that all these professors of the religion of Christ were volunteers.

10. SLAVONIANS. RUSSIANS. BASQUES.

The Slavonian race is Aryan, and numbers from seventy to eighty millions of people. Like all other races, the Russians are, of course, to some extent, a mixed race. In the course of their history they have taken in and assimilated a variety of Finnish and Turco-Finnish elements. Notwithstanding this process, the Slavonian type has maintained itself with remarkable

---
[1] *Missionary Anecdotes*, p. 169.

persistency. It comprises the Russians, Bulgarians, Illyrians, Croats, Servians, Poles, Hungarians, Lithuanians, Bohemians, Tchechs, Slovaks and Swabians.

They are of variable physical character. The influences of climate, and the degrees of civilisation and amount of education have established very great differences between the members of this family. They principally profess the religion of the Greek Church, but comprise about 800,000 Mohammedans, 2,000,000 Catholics, and under 1,000,000 Protestants.

The following is a letter from the remote and frozen Astrakan :—

'Dear Sister in Christ,
'You will not be surprised at my calling you so, for by this name are called those who are believers in Christ, and whom the Lord Himself is not ashamed to call His brethren, sisters, and friends. I do not doubt that amongst those beloved ones of the Lord are you, for whilst reading the precious lines of your journal, I said to myself, that she who edits it must be one of the Heavenly Father's children. One of those about whom the Lord was intreating His Father "that they all may be one." Therefore what a blessing that "we having been afar off have been made nigh through the blood of Christ." The little tracts you sent me have much cheered me in my almost incessant illness, which hinders my working for the spreading of God's word as I would. I will do all in my power to make your journal known, and increase its circulation, more especially as it holds an exclusively religious character; and I earnestly ask the Lord to enable you to stand firmly in the faith

and "to know nothing but Christ crucified." Being all the children of one Father we must all labour together for the spreading of His kingdom, both in word and in deed.'

RUSSIANS.

As a colporteur named Jacobson was wandering through the streets of Perm—a town in the neighbourhood of the Ural Mountains—an old man of eighty-five called him to enter the little cabin in which he sat. 'After examining the contents of my knapsack, with which he was much pleased, he told me that at fifty years of age he was occupied much in business between Moscow and Nijni. Up to that time he had thought little about God. Suddenly falling ill, he trembled at the prospect of death, and would fain have been delivered from the burden of his sins. A priest whom he consulted advised him to make a pilgrimage to the shrine of a well-known saint. By the goodness of God he was raised up, and he immediately went to the shrine. Here he stayed for some time, going through the various forms of devotion prescribed for him, but in vain. Another man, to whom he likewise told his case, gave him directions to pray with ceremonies different from the former, but the result was that the poor man's burden grew heavier than ever. After several years' trouble he obtained, by the kindness of a neighbour, a New Testament. Here he found that the Lord Jesus Christ had died for his sins and had been raised again for his justification, and the result was that he obtained peace through believing.'[1]

[1] *Report of the British and Foreign Bible Society* for 1884.

BULGARIANS.

The Bulgarians were originally Finns (Turanians), who issued from the Ural mountain district, and occupied countries belonging to Slavonic people, whose language and manners they assimilated. On the reconstruction of Europe after Charlemagne they became rulers of a considerable empire, but were subdued by the Turks about 1392.

A letter from Samokow, contained in the Report of the Religious Tract Society for 1882, states:—

'Although our Bulgarian nation, as you well know, has been nominally a Christian nation for more than ten centuries, yet sad as it is, the saving power of the Christian religion has been almost unknown to us, and so, as a rule, we have lived in darkness, without hope and without God in the world. One reason for this has been our having had no religious books in our language, nor men of God to teach us the truths of religion, and to lead our sinful souls to Jesus, the Saviour of all. But the Lord has looked in mercy upon us, and twenty years ago the voice of salvation through Jesus Christ began to be heard amongst us. Thank God it has not been as "a voice crying in the wilderness." Among many obstacles and persecutions it has gone on its way to purify the hearts of many of our countrymen, and to make their souls glad in a free and full salvation from sin and from death, through the blessed blood of Jesus.' Many of the native preachers and laymen among the Bulgarians now preach the doctrine of Christ in all its fulness.

MAGYARS.

These are the present Hungarians, who in the tenth century, after overrunning Eastern Europe, and even threatening France and Germany, settled in Hungary, and held fiercely and tenaciously to their local institutions and languages. They are cousins to the Finns of the Baltic and the Ottoman Turk, and have displayed, and still exhibit, very numerous instances of conversion to evangelical truth.

Mr. Millard, the agent of the British and Foreign Bible Society, gives us an instance in point. He writes:—'A young man called upon me to talk over his entering upon missionary service. "How did you come to the knowledge of the truth?" The reply was, "A colporteur happened to meet me. By his invitation I bought a New Testament. After a time I began to read it, and it made an impression on me which has never left me, but which, on the contrary, has grown on me until now I am a believer in Jesus—a humble though a very unworthy child of God."'

BOHEMIANS.

The westernmost extensions of the great Slavonic family are to be found in Bohemia, Carinthia, and Carniola. They show high cheek-bones like the Mongols, but their general appearance is much assimilated to that of the races by which they have been surrounded for many centuries. In Bohemia, the career of John Huss proves the aptitude of both nobles and people for the Gospel. There has never been wanting among them, those who at all hazards have opposed the sacramentarian practices of Rome, and advocated the simple Scriptural way of salvation.

John Gilch,—a Bohemian convert, in the beginning of the eighteenth century,—a Slav by birth, began his Christian life by contrition for sin, and then laid hold of and appropriated the pardoning word of Christ. He became an eminent confessor and martyr.

MORAVIANS.

Christian David, John Wesley's teacher, was a true Moravian, and therefore of Slavonic descent, though living and ministering among the German settlements at Hernnhut, in the year 1733. John Wesley gives an account of a sermon preached by David, which was made so useful to the hearer that Wesley afterwards attributed to it the entire change in his views and practice which took place from this epoch. The topic is 'Justification,' and the preacher says:— 'To him that believeth on God that justifieth the ungodly, his faith is counted for righteousness. See ye not that the foundation is nothing in us? There is no connection between God and the ungodly; there is no tie to unite them. They are altogether separate from each other. They have nothing in common. There is nothing less or more in the ungodly to join them to God. Works, righteousness, contrition? No. Ungodliness only. This then do, if you will lay a right foundation. Go straight to Christ with all your ungodliness. Tell Him, "Thou whose eyes are as a flame of fire, searching my heart, seest that I am ungodly. I plead nothing else. I do not say I am humble or contrite, but I am ungodly. Let Thy blood be the propitiation for me, for there is nothing in me but ungodliness."

'Labour then to believe with your whole heart. So shall you have redemption through the blood of Christ. So shall you be cleansed from all sin. So shall ye go on from strength to strength, being renewed day by day in righteousness and all true holiness.'[1]

The enterprise and success of the Moravians as missionaries are as well known as the simplicity of their tenets. We need not adduce illustrations or anecdotes of this. We avail ourselves of the forcible description by Dr. Chalmers: 'I cannot but remark how much effect and simplicity go together in the annals of Moravianism. The men of this truly interesting denomination address themselves exclusively to that principle of our nature on which the proper influence of Christianity turns; or, in other words, they take up the subject of the Gospel message—that message devised by Him who knew what was in man, and who therefore knew how to make the right and the suitable application to man.'[2]

In the Bible Society's Report for 1885, the following extract from a Bohemian colporteur's journal occurs:—

'This man daily read the Bible; he wept like a child when I read Ephesians ii. 1-10 to him, and explained to him that our salvation was free and complete, that we have merely to take it as the gift of God, and that we may and must come to Jesus just as we are. It was difficult to tear myself away from him, as he wanted to hear more and more of these precious things.'

[1] Gillies, p. 64. [2] *Astronomical Discourses*, p. 249.

BASQUES.

These original people, with their peculiar language, are an island as it were in the midst of the population of Europe. They alone have held their own in the presence of all invaders, and occupy now the same district which they held in Roman times. They are trustworthy, loyal and industrious, but ignorant and prejudiced. A mission carried on by the Protestants of the south of France into the recesses of the Pyrenees encounters no other opposition than arises from the alienation caused by ignorance of the love and work of Christ.

There are three versions of the Scriptures in different dialects in the Basque language. There is a scanty evangelical literature in the language, and some conversions are recorded in the Basque provinces, notably among the Guipuscoans at San Sebastian.

II. SCANDINAVIANS AND TEUTONS.

The great Germanic race may be conveniently divided into Germans, Scandinavians, and English, all belonging to that branch of the human family called by Cuvier Caucasians, since styled Aryans. The oval-shaped head, fine proportions, and regular features, distinguish the typical forms of these well-known peoples.

The Danes, Swedes, and Norwegians are also Teutons, a vigorous, hardy race, with large, sinewy frames, fine complexion, most frequently blue eyes, light hair, and sanguine temperament.

In the pre-Christian beliefs of all Germany and the northern nations there was no semblance of a gospel. Odin, of whom our language and folk-lore still retain traces, was the chief divinity. Dr. Burn characterises the creed as follows: 'To the Northmen every cause in nature was a divinity. He heard some god in almost every sound, he saw one in almost every change. The thunder was the rattle of Thor's chariot, the lightning the flash of his hammer, swiftly hurled from his strong hand; the wind was Sleipner, the fleet steed of Odin; the dew, foam from the bit of the horse at night. When the hard winter crust of the earth began to thaw it was Rind yielding to the rough wooing of her persistent lover; when in spring the early flowers bloomed, and the first bird was seen, it was Gerd cajoled by Skirnia to listen to the addresses of Frey. As the yearly wave of verdure washed up the hillside, and the herdsman drove his cattle from the lowland meadow to the green uplands, Sif was beside him with her yellow hair; as the farmer looked at his fields covered with rich grain he blessed the nuptials of Odin and Frigg.

'The fisherman, rowing his boat through the dancing waves saw in each of them a daughter of Oeger; listening on shore to the loud tumult of the angry sea he heard the wrathful clamour of those fickle maidens. The huntsmen were haunted by a divine presence in the silent deeps of the forest; the child as he looked upon the rainbow was told by his mother that that was the trembling bridge by which the gods crossed from heaven to earth. When the long days of summer were over, and winter with its darkness and cold had come, the sad tale of the death of the bright and good Baldur was told at many a fireside, and many a tear shed over the unhappy fate of that best beloved of all the gods. The whole world was divine to the old Northman.'[1]

The Teutonic individuality is surely well-displayed in Luther; and his satisfaction in discovering the doctrine of Christ's atonement, after vain efforts to obtain peace without it, is common knowledge. He sang, '"There is no man who has died for our sins but Jesus Christ the Son of God." When by the Spirit of God I understood those words, when I learnt how the justification of the sinner proceeds from God's free mercy by the way of faith, then I felt myself born again as a new man, and I entered by an open door into the very paradise of God.'

Old Kilian, a German colporteur for the Bible Society, who died in 1881, having been born with the century, affords a good instance of the suitableness of the doctrine of Christ's atonement to the Teutonic mind. The Report of the Bible Society for 1885 thus records his experience after his infancy:—

'Being now an orphan, he was sent by his guardians to learn the trade of a tailor, in following which he some years later settled at Bremen, where he married, began business on his own account, and was in fairly comfortable circumstances. But, accustomed to seek happiness in religion, he realised that the most strict observance of his religious duties gave him no satisfaction. He had no inward peace. He knew of Jesus, but only to dread Him. He did not know the

---

[1] *Faiths of the World*, p. 260.

purpose of His incarnation, death, and resurrection. Kilian passed through a long period of anguish at this time, but he often sought light and relief by pouring out his soul to God in prayer. A hymn of Lavater's, breathing a desire after holiness and indifference to the things of the world, at one time gave him comfort.

A NORWEGIAN PASTOR.

"At length, in 1828," he goes on to say, "the Lord sent an evangelist to my house, who said to me: 'It is true you know *about* Jesus, but you do not really know Him!' and he recommended me to read the Scriptures. Immediately I conferred not with flesh and blood, but accepted Christ, and found that which I had for so long a period ardently desired. I found God in Christ, and now nothing is dearer to me than He. I find all in Him." Kilian was then twenty-seven years of age, and he set himself at once to make known to others what a rich treasure he had found. "From that time I wished to tell, I felt I could tell, to all the world how good it is to be in Christ."[1]

A recent narrative published by the Religious Tract Society shows that the Norsk nature possesses the same aptitude for the essential truth of the Christian system that we have observed in other races.

One afternoon a lady visitor in a large hospital was reading the Bible, and speaking to the patients who had gathered round the fire in the men's ward. As she rose to take leave she turned to a Norwegian sailor lad who had attracted her attention, and laid her hand upon his shoulder as she put to him the question, 'Marius, do you think your sins are forgiven?' Her question raised thoughts in the head of Marius which he could not put away. He had been in the habit of running away at the mention of a serious word, and would have done so now, but for the gentle touch of the lady's hand. Still, put it from him as he would, the thought of those unforgiven sins sorely troubled him. In his distress he asked for a Bible; one in his own tongue was given him by the lady who nursed the sick in that hospital, and now Marius' whole time was spent in searching it for the one great longing of his heart was to find peace with God; but the more he read the more he saw how guilty he was in the sight of Him who 'is of purer eyes than to behold iniquity.' In his outward life he had not been worse than most lads, but now he was learning something of his ruined state by nature. Very lonely in that hospital, and keeping his struggles to himself, Marius had no other teacher than God's own Word brought home to his heart by the Holy Spirit. One day, when his heart was weighed down at finding no comfort, no rest for his soul, he came to these words, 'But now the righteousness of God without the law is manifested, being witnessed by the law and the prophets; even the righteousness of God which is by faith of Jesus Christ, unto all and upon all them that believe; for there is no difference, for all have sinned and come short of the glory of God, being justified freely by His grace, through the redemption that is in Christ Jesus; whom God hath set forth to be a propitiation through faith in His blood, to declare His righteousness for the remission of sins that are past, through the forbearance of God, to declare, I say, at this time His righteousness, that He might be just, and the justifier of him which believeth in Jesus.'

Then, to use his own words, Marius 'saw it all.' Yes, he saw that though he had no righteousness of his own, and was guilty before God, Jesus had borne his sins, and had paid his debts upon the cross. Who can describe the joy that filled the poor lad's heart, and the love with which he clung to his newly-found Saviour?[1]

> 'O Faith! thou workest miracles
>   Upon the hearts of men,
> Choosing thy home in those same hearts,
>   We know not how or when.

---

[1] *Every Week Tracts*, No. 941.

> To one the deepest doctrines look
>   So naturally true,
> That when he learns the lesson first
>   He hardly thinks it new.'

12. ENGLISH.

Never was race more blended than that which now bears the English name. In sketching its varied pedigree we are carried back to the darkest of the dark ages of the past, and obtain glimpses also of a pre-Aryan, dark, short, barbarous people. Then came the successive immigrations of Kelt and Teuton, Frisian, Jute and Dane, all wavelets of the great Aryan flood; and after them the Saxons, from the same source, but with language, habit and manners modified by residence in North Germany and on the Baltic. Then came the Normans, a Scandinavian and Gaulish people, so that the original stock has been constantly modified, and we can only claim to be a mixture of Anglo-Saxon to the extent of about one-half. Yet the result is a type called the English character: different from the more volatile Gauls on the one hand, and the slower Teutons on the other.

A characteristic specimen of the British mind is afforded by Thomas Bilney, a Cambridge student, martyred for the faith in the year 1531. He may be selected as a fair specimen of a thoughtful, careful, honest English scholar. He came under religious concern, which recourse to the Church and to the words of the teachers failed to satisfy. After some delay, he sought and obtained possession of a forbidden Greek Testament; he hastened to his room and shut himself in with the dangerous treasure. It is related that as he opened it his eye caught the words, 'This is a faithful saying and worthy of all acceptation, that Christ Jesus came into the world to save sinners, of whom I am chief.' This was the truth which his soul and his heart needed.

He said, 'At last I have found Jesus. Yes, Jesus Christ saves.' He was satisfied and happy in the possession of this spiritual treasure throughout the rest of his short life, and at its dreadful and cruel termination by martyrdom at Norwich.

We may adduce the testimony of John Wesley, as one whose experience gives absolute value to his judgment, and who was a true Englishman. In reply to a correspondent he says :—

'From the year 1725 to 1729 I preached much, but I saw no fruit of my labour. Indeed, it could not be that I should ; for I neither laid the foundation of repentance, nor of believing the Gospel ; taking it for granted that all to whom I preached were believers, and that many of them needed no repentance. From the year 1729 to 1734, laying a deeper foundation of repentance, I saw a little fruit. But it was only a little, and no wonder. For I did not preach faith in the blood of the covenant. From 1734 to 1738, speaking more of faith in Christ, I saw more fruit of my preaching and visiting from house to house, than ever I had done before, though I know not if any of those who were outwardly reformed were inwardly and thoroughly converted to God. From 1738 to this time, speaking continually of Jesus Christ, laying Him only for the foundation of the whole building, making Him all in all, the first and the last, preaching wholly on this plan, "The kingdom of God is at hand, repent ye and believe the gospel," the word of God ran as fire among the stubble, it was glorified more and more, multitudes crying out "What must we do to be saved?" and afterwards witnessing "By grace we are saved through faith."[1]

The autobiographical statement of the Rev. Thomas Adam, rector of Winteringham in Lincolnshire, a grave, intelligent clergyman, will serve for another instance of a very numerous class.

About the year 1740 he was fulfilling his routine of duties with exactness, living so as to satisfy himself and stand well with the world. He became acquainted with the writings of Mr. Law and the mystics. These induced within him the desire for peace with God, but showed him not the way of its attainment. After stumbling for a year or two amidst theological difficulties, consulting commentators in vain, striving for inward satisfaction so strenuously that his friends deemed him to be insane, he emerged into the glorious liberty and divine peace of the Gospel.

The process is narrated by his biographer Stillingfleet as follows:—'One morning in his study, being much distressed on the subject, he fell down upon his knees to God in prayer, spread his case before the Divine Majesty and goodness, imploring Him to pity his distress, and to guide him by His Holy Spirit into the right understanding of His own truth. When he arose from his supplication, he took the Greek Testament and set himself down to read the first six chapters of the Epistle to the Romans sincerely desirous to be taught of God, and to receive

[1] *Gillie's Collection*, ii. 103.

in the simplicity of a child the word of His revelation; when, to his unspeakable comfort and astonishment, his difficulties vanished—a most clear and satisfactory light was given him into this great subject. He saw the doctrine of justification by Jesus Christ alone, through faith, to be the great object of the Gospel, the highest display of the Divine perfections, the happiest relief for his burdened conscience, and the most powerful principle of all constant and unfeigned holiness of heart and life. He was rejoiced exceedingly, he found peace and comfort spring up in his mind; his conscience was purged from guilt through the atoning blood of Christ, and his heart set at liberty to run the way of God's commands without fear, in a spirit of filial love and holy delight; and from that hour he began to preach salvation through faith in Jesus Christ alone, to man, by nature and practice lost and condemned under the law, and, as his own expression is, always a sinner.'[1]

John Nelson, a Yorkshire stonemason, came under the influence of John Wesley's first sermon in Moorfields. In his journal, after describing his previous confusion of mind and trouble of soul for want of definite ground of faith, he describes the exact effect of saving truth as follows: 'I was like a wandering bird cast out of the nest, till Mr. John Wesley came to preach his first sermon in Moorfields. Oh, that was a blessed morning to my soul! As soon as he got upon the stand he stroked back his hair, and turned his face toward where I stood, and I thought fixed his eye upon me. When he had done I said, "This man can tell the secret of my heart; he hath not left me

[1] *Life of Adam*, by Dr. Stillingfleet.

there, but he hath showed the remedy, even the blood of Jesus. Then was my soul filled with consolation, through hope that God, for Christ's sake, would save me, neither did I doubt in such a manner any more."[1]

Scotland can afford us instances from the first dawn of historic literature to the present day, and in all the varieties of its social life. The case of Thomas Halyburton, Professor of Theology at St. Andrews, at the beginning of the last century will suffice. He is speaking of his own conversion at the age of twenty-four, and says: 'That which yielded me this relief was discovery of the Lord, as manifested in the Word. . . . . I was fully satisfied that not only was there forgiveness of sin and justification by free grace, "through the redemption that is in Jesus, whom God has set forth to be a propitiation through faith in His blood, to declare the righteousness for the remission of sins that are past, through the forbearance of God"; but, moreover, I saw with wonder and delight in some measure how God, by this means, might be just in justifying even the ungodly who believe in Jesus. Then was I ravished with delight when made to see that the God in whom a little before I thought there was no hope for me, or any sinner in my case, might not only pardon, but without prejudice to His justice or other attributes be just and justifying even the ungodly.'

We quote sentiments implying the same processes from the statements of two Englishmen of profound thought and large scholarship. The first, Archbishop Leighton, says:—' Where, if not in Christ, is the power that can persuade a sinner to return, *that can bring*

---

[1] Nelson's *Life and Journals*, p. 18.

home a heart to God?' on which the comment of the second, Samuel Taylor Coleridge, is, ' Common mercies of God, though they have a leading faculty to repentance (Rom. ii. 4), yet the rebellious heart will not be led by them. The judgments of God, public or personal, though they ought to drive us to God, yet the heart, unchanged, runs the further from God. Leave Christ out, I say, and all other means work not this way. By the phrase, "In Christ," I understand all the supernatural aids vouchsafed and conditionally promised in the Christian dispensation ; . . . aids, observe, therefore, not by the will of man alone, but neither without the will.'[1]

The ready acceptance of the Gospel in the manner indicated in the extracts contained in this volume of course does not displace the fact of the natural alienation of the human mind from God. Our argument is, that where this alienation is overcome, it is conquered only by a real apprehension of the love and work of Christ, and by this alone, and we have adduced cumulative evidence in support of this contention. But we do not desire to burden the reader with details of examples so familiar. Indeed, if the appeal were made to British Christians, we might anticipate and summarise the response in the words of a well-known hymn :—

' I asked them whence their victory came ;
They with united breath
Ascribe their conquests to the Lamb,
Their triumph to His death.'

---

[1] *Aids to Reflection*, ed. 1843, vol. i. p. 114.

13. KELTS.

There are two divisions of modern Kelts, one, the smaller, comprising the Highlanders of Scotland, and the Irish, the Gaels; the other the Bretons, and the Welsh (Kymric).

Among the first authentic notices of the Kelts, after the Romans had left, were the narratives of the missionaries *to* them, and immediately afterwards *by* them. In the curious rhymed creed of St. Patrick we find something which looks like evidence in favour of our proposition :—

> 'Christ with me—Christ before me,
> Christ behind me—Christ within me,
> Christ at my right—Christ at my left,
> Christ is the foot—Christ is the chariot,
> Christ is the ship.
> Christ is the heart of every man who thinks of me,
> Christ is the mouth of every man that speaks to me,
> Christ in every eye that sees me,
> Christ in every ear that hears me.'

A thorough Irishman was John Walsh; a Romanist a scholar, a gentleman. In 1748 he heard one of Wesley's itinerants preaching on the parade ground at Limerick. The light of divine truth illumined his understanding, and the attractive power of Christ crucified affected his heart. He forsook the creed of his fathers, and became a devoted laborious preacher throughout his native isle. He is described as running through the country like a flame of fire, preaching constantly twice a day. Wesley says concerning him, ' I do not remember ever to have known a preacher who in so few years as he remained upon earth was an instrument of converting so many sinners.'

The natives of Wales are mainly Kelts. Their poetic ardour and religious fervour are manifested in the mode of their reception of the Gospel. It is related by the celebrated preacher of the eighteenth century, Daniel Rowlands, of Langeiche, that on one occasion, whilst reading the Litany at the Sunday morning service, as he uttered these words, 'By Thine agony and bloody sweat, by Thy cross and passion, by Thy precious death and burial, by Thy glorious resurrection and ascension, and by the coming of the Holy Ghost,' his whole soul was entranced, and his stalwart frame trembled, a thrill suddenly went through the assembly, and every knee and every mind was bent in prayer.

During the religious revival in Wales in the year 1860, numbers of persons present at the ordinary services of the Church came forward in dozens [1] under strong mental excitement, acknowledging their sins and obtained peace by exercising faith in the merits of Christ.[2] A correspondent of Mr. Venn writes: 'Having heard from the pulpit of the unsearchable riches of Christ, we desire to receive them, and this has led us to our knees, to seek and to enjoy.'[3]

It would be easy to multiply instances.

---

[1] *The Celts*, by Dr. Maclear, p. 96.
[2] Venn's *Revival in Wales*, p. 31.
[3] *Ib.* p. 121.

A GREEK WOMAN

14. GREEKS.

The Greeks, in the time of the Apostle Paul, and for ages afterwards, were distinguished for the fulness with which they presented man in his natural state, polished to the utmost by poetry, art, and refinement, but abounding in weakness and vice. Their language is the most beautiful, rich, and harmonious ever spoken or written, their eyes were accustomed to the most beautiful conceptions of the sculptor and painter.

Perhaps the old Greek religion came nearer than any other to simple nature worship; but the ancient images in which the powers of nature were represented or symbolised soon absorbed among the common people the regard originated by the air, earth, and sea. At the time that Christianity was first brought to the Grecians by the Apostle Paul, their national religion had become an idolatry of the most extensive kind, and their religious symbols were those of every evil thing.

Dr. Milligan, writing of the religion of Greece, and of its failure to advance with history or culture, says: 'Its want of all traces of a true theology, its puerilities, its inability to throw light upon the problem of life, its mocking silence when questioned by the serious mind, not only showed its impotence, but created a gulf between it and the actions and thoughts of men which told that its day was passing.'[1]

How did they receive the new religion from Palestine? Certainly as a novel idea. 'May we know

[1] *Faiths of the World*, p 210.

what this new doctrine whereof thou speakest is? For thou bringest certain strange things to our ears, we would know therefore what these things mean.' 'Howbeit certain men clave unto him and believed, among whom also was Dionysius the Areopagite.'

Yet these were the people who, when Christ was preached unto them by the Apostle Paul, 'were glad, and glorified the word of God,'[1] and who, in vain and voluptuous Corinth, could be addressed by the same apostle as 'sanctified in Christ Jesus,' and as 'called into the fellowship of Jesus Christ our Lord.'[2]

The present government of Greece is opposed to the spread of the Scriptures, but in spite of this the sale of them by the colporteurs to the people is large and continuous. The Greek New Testament is, however, adopted in the Government elementary schools.

The Albanians are of Aryan race, and it was to these, in Illyria, that the Gospel was preached by St. Paul.[3]

15. THE LATIN RACES.

The Latin races are descendants of an Aryan migration of unknown date, which made its way through Asia Minor, across the Hellespont, and spent its force along the shores and on the islands of the Mediterranean Sea. From the Aryan stream diverged the Greeks, and afterwards the Latins; and from the latter arose the great Roman Empire, which embraced the whole world known to learning in the days of our Lord. It is well known how, on the breaking up of

---

[1] Acts xiii. 48.   [2] 1 Cor. i. 2, 9.
[3] Acts xvii. 19, 34.

the empire, the Italian, French, Spanish, and many other minor states and languages of mixed population and language, branched off, and became more and more divergent, until in the Middle Ages we find the Latin race along the southern line of the Mediterranean in distinct nationalities, and the Teutons, forming their northern boundary; thus dividing the civilised world into Latin and German; so that, some centuries before the Norman conquest of England, the Latin races had become placed much as we find them at present: the Latins of France, with some Keltic admixture; those of Spain, with Arabian additions. The Italians, a mixed race having a Latin base with Teutonic additions, on the north, and Greek and Moorish on the south.

ITALIANS.

The ground-work of Roman heathenism was a traditional idolatry, and its ruling manifestation, force, as displayed by human nature. They worshipped twelve gods (the great gods), and a very great number of subordinate deities, in groups which represent the power of nature, and the passions and characteristics of man. This was raised to state establishment, and elaborated with rites, ceremonies, temples, and priests so as to cover the whole country, but with very slight hold on the educated classes.

The Roman religion at the time the Gospel was first preached at Rome consisted mainly in a public recognition of the old gods of Greece, with the addition to them of Roman attributes; this was merely the public state creed, not held by the upper classes, but avowed by the superstitious and ignorant populace, though repudiated by the cultured people. The latter displayed only a dismal, comfortless scepticism.

In 1534 Antonio della Baglia of Siena, a young scholar of elegant literary accomplishments, a professor and lecturer there, studied St. Augustine, and through the Holy Scriptures, received thoroughly the doctrine of justification by faith, and found in it a power which (as D'Aubigné says), 'was to him the warrant of its truth.' He said: 'Since He in whom the Godhead dwells has so lovingly poured out His blood for our salvation, we must not doubt of the favour of Heaven upon all who turn their souls towards Jesus crucified, and bind themselves to Him with thorough confidence to be delivered from evil and receive forgiveness for their sins.'[1]

One of the literary ornaments of the Renaissance period in Italy was unquestionably Olympia Morata, born at Ferrara in 1526, and educated amidst a galaxy of art and genius at the court of Ferrara. Distinguished by superior endowments, attainments, and taste in poetry and literature, she read, enjoyed, and commented on the writings of the great men of Greece and Rome, and obtained the applause of a wide circle of admirers. In the midst of fascinating life she dared, in the exercise of her literary freedom, to look at the doctrine of Justification by Faith, then exciting so much commotion in Germany, and became a convert to evangelical doctrine. She writes, as her own confession and as agreeing with her inmost thought: 'God so loved the world that He gave His own Son to die for it. The Son so loved

---

[1] *Reformation in Europe*, Book vii.

the world that He voluntarily yielded up His life for it upon the cross. He who puts his trust in Jesus Christ, the Prince of Peace, shall live for ever.' This was the groundwork of the happiness and usefulness of her remarkable life.

Modern Rome and Italy furnish numerous similar instances in all ranks and classes.

The Reports of Mrs. Wall respecting the Medical Mission at Rome give numerous instances in corroboration of the argument. I quote only one, and that from the Report for the year 1887 :—

'One morning, while conversing with the patients at the Medical Mission, a peasant woman from the hills, apparently a stranger, who was sitting waiting for the doctor, said to me, "I am so glad to be here again, signora; you do not perhaps remember me, but I was in Rome in the spring, and not being well, I was recommended to come and see this doctor. You taught me a verse of a hymn which I have never forgotten; it begins, 'Look to the Lamb of God.' I repeated it over and over again until I could sing it. Ever since then, all through the summer, when at work in the fields, these words have been such a comfort to me." While repeating the verse I noticed the tears were running down her cheeks. At last she said: "You must excuse me, signora, but I never can say this without crying, it is so beautiful."'

An agent of the Bible Society narrates the following instance of conversion among the modern Italians :—

'There came to the fair at P—— a good many small traders, among whom was a good-looking youth, called Alphonso, a jeweller, who set up his bench opposite mine. I was grieved to hear him swear horribly, and as I felt some sympathy for him, I watched for an opportunity of speaking to him. I had not long to wait, for next day he came and asked if I had any romances. On my showing him the Bible he laughed, and put it down, saying: "Give that to the priest, for I do not pretend to have any religion." I could make no impression on him, and he left me. In the evening I met him, and we went to sup together. He said: "You think me so wicked as not to believe in God?" I replied: "You yourself told me that, and then you often blaspheme Him." He said he had often tried to give up the habit of swearing, but in vain; besides, he said he had led a very immoral life. We conversed together for more than three hours. I based my remarks on Isaiah xlii. 7, telling him of the Saviour's love for sinners, and reminding him that we must one day stand before Him as our Judge. Surely the Lord is with us when we endeavour to make Him known to others. It was He who spoke to Gerola, not I; and near the end of his conversation I could see his eyes were full of tears.

'On the morning of the next day I went to visit him early, and as soon as he saw me he thanked me warmly for all I had said to him the evening before, telling me he had not slept, but that it was a great comfort to him to think that the thief on the cross was forgiven, "because I have placed my confidence in Jesus, and been pardoned too."'[1]

[1] *Bible Conquests*, p. 201.

SPANIARDS AND PORTUGUESE.

The Spaniard is the result of original Keltic, then Gothic, then Moorish conquest, with influence from the propinquity of Basques on the north and Italians on the south and east.

In the centre of Spain we are reminded of the old Roman type, in the southern, of Moorish, but there are at least five distinct nationalities still observable in the peninsula.

A true Spaniard was Dr. Constantine Ponca de la Fuenta, Canon of the Cathedral of Seville, and the most popular preacher of his age in all Spain. In 1556 he published his *Confessions of a Sinner*, and it is adduced here because it was the result, not of communications with promoters of the Reformed doctrine, but of his own personal study of the Gospel. In that he says, in addressing the Lord: 'Hast Thou not given satisfaction for that which Thou hadst not done? Is not Thy blood a sacrifice for the pardon of all the sins of the human race? Is it not that the treasures of Thy grace avail more for my welfare than all Adam's sin and misery for my ruin? Hast Thou not wept on my account, asking pardon for me? and Thy Father, has He not heard Thee? Who then can remove from my heart its confidence in such promises?'

Juan Valdes, who died in 1541, was a Castilian of pure blood. In his tractate on the fundamentals of Christian doctrine,[1] he thus writes: 'I should pre-

---

[1] Translated by J. T. Betts. Published by Hodder and Stoughton. 1881.

scribe that the Gospel should be preached in the very words in which, as shown by St. Paul, it was preached by the Apostles ; where he states that it is an apostle's duty to go through the world as an ambassador from Christ, telling men (2 Cor. v. 20), " Now then we are ambassadors for Christ, as though God did beseech you by us ; we pray you in Christ's stead, be ye reconciled to God. For He hath made Him to be sin for us, who knew no sin ; that we might be made the righteousness of God in Him ;" as though they should say, On behalf of Christ, we beg you to hold yourselves as pardoned by God ; as reconciled with God, as just, and as friends of God ; and, in order that you may know you may safely do it, know that Christ, who never knew what sin was, has been made sin by God. I do not say a sinner, but sin ; laying upon Him all our sins, past and future, to mantle us in His righteousness.'

A modern Spanish conversion is thus related by Mr. Moreton :—

'One of our best members told me the history of his conversion. He was brought by a friend to our services ; and although he cared little about religion he became interested, bought a Bible, and resolved curiously enough to read it right through from Genesis to Revelation ; but the story of the fall and expulsion from Eden filled him with dismay. The thought of death had always been distasteful to him, but now to learn he was ruined by sin made him despair, and he threw the book aside. Some time after he took it up again, and the Gospels gave him hope, whereupon he felt encouraged to follow on to know the Lord, and continued to attend the services with increasing interest, until one day he received a tract at Villa Nova Chapel.[1] This brought before him the idea of communion with God, and filled him with a blessed influence far beyond any of his former experiences. Henceforward he has run well, and bears a bright testimony for the Master.'[2]

In the Report of the Religious Tract Society for 1882 we find material testimony in a letter written by a young lady to a friend, who sent her a copy of the *Sinner's Friend:* ' I really cannot find words to express thanks to you for the little book you so kindly sent me. It points out exactly the verses of Scripture most appropriate to my case. My fears are taken away, and a sinner like me is made to rejoice that God sent His only begotten Son to die for us, and that His blood cleanses us from all sin.'

The Spaniards, after their usual fashion, intensify their utterances into proverbs. To understand the following saying it is necessary to bear in mind, first, that St. Augustine is the representative of evangelical dogma, and secondly, that the savoury portion in the *olla*, the national dish of Spain, is the lump of bacon which is cooked with the stew. The proverb is,

Sermo sin Agostino,
Olla sin tocino,

A sermon without Augustine is an olla without bacon.

As a recent instance we quote the following :—
'About ten years ago a native of Spain, Don Francisco Previ, was a patient at the Royal Oph-

---

[1] *Orais* (' Do you pray ?'), by Bishop Ryle.
[2] *Religious Tract Society Report*, 1882, p. 56.

thalmic Hospital, Moorfields. At the same period a young English lady, Miss Emily Murray, was a worker in the Bible flower mission in connection with Miss Macpherson's Home of Industry, Spitalfields, and in that capacity used to pay a weekly visit to the patients in the hospital. She met Senor Previ, and presented him with a Spanish Bible and a text-card. The card bore the words from Paul's First Epistle to Timothy (ii. 5), " For there is one God, and one Mediator between God and men, the Man Christ Jesus.' These words sank into his heart, and brought peace. He studied his Bible, and his conversion became complete.'

16. FRENCH.

The French are Aryans of the Celtic stock, with large Teutonic and Roman mixture. The characteristics of the Teuton prevail in Northern France, of the Romans in the south, the Danes in Normandy, the Kelt in Brittany.

France, in all her varied religious history, has never been wanting in men of ability and faith who have proclaimed and exemplified the doctrines of evangelical Christianity. Calvin and the early Reformers, Pascal and the Jansenists, Fénelon and the Quietists, the Huguenots and Camisards, Vinet and Merle D'Aubigné, rise to the memory as representative men. The journals inform us that the religious lectures which are the most popular are those which set forth the atoning work of Christ.[2] Travellers, especially in France, can testify that both in Catholic or

---

[1] The *Missionary News*, January 1886, p. 3.
[2] *Religious Condition of Christendom*, Berlin, 1857, p. 455.

FRENCH TYPES.

Protestant pulpits this is the topic most acceptable, and draws the largest audiences. Indeed, full proof of our proposition is shown by the history of Augustinian doctrines in France, and by authenticated modern experience to the same effect.

'A colporteur in France was menaced with real danger on entering a farm-yard belonging to a gentleman's seat which lay in his way. The proprietor was standing in the court surrounded by his workmen and servants. He suffered the stranger to draw nigh, that he might know what was wanted. Upon hearing he was a vendor of books he broke into a rage, and exclaimed that the times of the Inquisition were being revived; that the agents of the Jesuits penetrated into every house to plague people, and to denounce them to the police, if they did not receive them well. "Hallo, my friends, give it to this canting fellow, and if he does not take himself off set the dogs on him!" Our friend stood this broadside without being disturbed. When he was going to explain what he was, a young man stepped between the gentleman and the colporteur, and said to the former, "I hope you will forgive me, sir, if I venture to say you are mistaken. This good man is not what you suppose, for in the first place, he is a Protestant."

'"Ha! a Protestant, he is not a Jesuit. What does he want?"

'"What he wants, sir, is to do you good, as he has done me. Look here, he sold me this little book," said he, drawing from the pocket under his blouse a little Testament, "and I assure you what he says is true. I mean that if any one reads this book and prays, he is perfectly happy. I speak from experience. I am a poor peasant, very ignorant in everything, and yet that has not prevented my understanding that God so loved me as to give His Son to save me; and ever since I have believed that I have been the happiest of men."

'"And have you learnt that out of this book all by yourself?"

'"Yes, sir."

'"And how did you manage it?"

'"I followed the advice of this good man. I read the Gospel and prayed and prayed and read the Gospel."

'"Is this all true that he tells me, bookseller?"

'"Perfectly correct, sir, and his history is mine."'[1]

We read that 'in the Department de l'Oise a colporteur had great cause for joy. He met a farmer's wife who hailed him as a messenger of peace. This poor woman, who was celebrated as a devotee, was very much burdened with the feeling of her sins. To attain peace, she confessed every week, and had made pilgrimages to every virgin and saint of the country; she had covered her rooms with their pictures, yet she said she was in horrible anguish. When she heard our friend he inspired her with so much confidence that she opened her heart to him. He spoke strongly of the uselessness of the vain practices employed by the woman, and quoted several passages of Scripture. He was understood much better than he expected. After this first conversation she bought the Bible, and spent the whole night reading it. After the second conversation this anguished soul addressed directly the Saviour of sinners. When the colporteur went to the house the third time all the images of madonnas

[1] *Bible Conquests*, p. 180.

and saints had disappeared, the Bible alone had the place of honour, and what is still better, it held the first place in a heart that had been consoled, purified, and rejoiced by it.'[1]

The Report of the Religious Tract Society for 1886 contains the following communication from a coal miner at Fraisnes:—

'I write you a few lines in order to show you what is going on amongst us. We are a few poor sinners who have learned to know our Lord and Saviour Jesus Christ, and having received His grace and pardon, and the sweet peace He gives to those who seek Him, we are anxious to tell what we feel is important. So great is the joy of the lost sinner who has been the slave to his passions, when through Jesus, though still a sinner, he becomes a sinner saved, washed in the blood of the Lamb, still a slave, but a slave of God. It is a great joy to the Christian to be able to tell to his former companions in misery that God wishes them also to be reconciled. And, like the Samaritan woman, we are happy to go and tell to the inhabitants of the villages round us that they should go to Jesus, the Christ and the Saviour, in order to obtain the pardon of their sins.'

Mr. McAll relates, among the incidents of his mission work at Paris, that a French country gentleman, who had come to Paris to enjoy its worldly pleasures, heard M. Th. Monod preach, and became interested, read the New Testament for the first time, became a regular attendant, and came gradually to a knowledge of the truth.

'As the time drew near for his departure,' says the

[1] *Bible Conquests*, p. 184.

narrator, 'he was anxious I should visit him in his pleasant country home, to preach to the peasants of his native village, but most of all that we might ponder over the Word of God. He said: "I never heard these things before—all so new. I never saw a Bible before. I went to Paris for pleasure—a deist; believing nothing. Death, I thought, was annihilation; religion, useful, but false; and Jesus a myth. You have taught me that God became man. I have learned from Adolphe Monod's book that we need a sacrifice to cleanse away our sin. Now I believe in Jesus Christ!"

'On the Sunday he gathered all his neighbours together in his farmer's kitchen. The large chair of the time of Louis XV. was taken in for the preacher, and all the village met to hear the Word. He said, "I am anxious that my people should hear the Gospel. Now, don't preach a grand sermon to them, for they won't understand you. But I want you to talk to them about the Lord Jesus Christ. Tell them how He, the great God, became a servant, and that they may all become citizens of heaven."'

At a recent meeting of the McAll Mission in Paris a big burly man in working dress stood up and asked leave to speak. When it was granted, he began in rather a startling fashion: 'I am a miracle, a supernatural phenomenon! I want to tell you what God has done for me. I am a Parisian, and as a youth was "*un mauvais garnement.*" As a soldier I was so unruly that I was sent into a disciplinary corps in Algiers to be reformed, and when my time expired I returned to Paris worse than when I left it. I sank so low that I was an object of loathing to myself and of disgust to my friends; they could not see me, and I dared not look at myself. The only person who cared to see me was the publican, and he only when I had money in my pocket. In this abject condition I went into the *réunion* Rue de Rivoli, and heard about the love of God. The text, "God so loved the world," arrested me, it gave me hope. I continued to follow the meetings, and one day I heard, "Jesus Christ came into the world to save sinners;" that soothed my conscience and gave me peace. From that day I was a new man. I am not rich, but by work I have enough, and I declare to you that I am a happy, contented man. I don't say I have no troubles, but I know to whom I may carry them.' Then in earnest, eloquent words he urged the audience to follow him in believing the Gospel that had raised him from lower than the brutes to the position of a child of God.[1]

We conclude our survey of the peoples of the world, in regard to their acceptance of the Gospel, by an enumeration of the translations of the book which tells mankind of the love and work of Christ, the Bible, into the vernacular spoken languages and dialects of man. This, according to the valuable summary prepared by Dr. Robert Cust in 1886,[2] is as follows:—

I. Europe	78
II. Asia	105
III. Africa	62
IV. America	38
V. Oceania	41
Total	324

---

[1] McAll, *Mission Magazine*, October, 1886.
[2] *Language Illustrated by Bible Translation*, Trübner & Co.

CHAPTER VIII.

CONCLUSIONS.

> Oh, how shall I, whose native sphere
>   Is dark, whose mind is dim,
> Before the Ineffable appear,
> And on my naked spirit bear
>   The uncreated beam?
>
> There is a way for man to rise
>   To His sublime abode,
> An offering, and a sacrifice,
> A Holy Spirit's energies,
>   An Advocate with God.—BINNEY.

BELIEF includes, as is well known, two elements: an intellectual one, mere assent, and an emotional one, conviction. The first may be produced without the second, and in that case it has no power, indeed no operation. The cases of mere intellectual, dry, emotionless assent to the most personally important truths, either as regarding this world or the next are too numerous to require argument. It is not intensity of assent, or the multiplication of those who assent, which has ruled the world, but the intensity of conviction. The power of the idea to fulfil some felt need and accomplish some desired effect, is the mode in which its strength is shown and used.

What we here maintain is, that everywhere, and in every race of mankind the reception of the Gospel method of forgiveness and salvation through Christ, apprehended by the aid of the promised influence of God the Holy Spirit has produced conviction.

Many persons, however, maintain that natural religion would suffice for the man's religious wants. They appear to consider that Theism, and the belief in the immortality of the soul, are the two dogmas which are sufficient for the needs of our race. The experience of the missionary everywhere, however, is, that though he has tried these considerations on the Pagan mind, yet he has never thereby obtained any useful result in a change of life. But on his opening the New Testament and reading the account of the Saviour's suffering, the heart of the hearer begins to swell, and his tears to flow as he realises that all this was done for him.

We have seen that the message of a full acceptable atonement is welcomed by the universal conscience. History and experience attest the reasonableness and congruity of a vicarious offering. No further evidence is required than the consciousness of the individual. This grounds the successful appeal of the missionary.[1] When the work of Christ in assuming the guilt of the sinner is explained to a heathen, he has no difficulty in understanding it. He regards it as quite reasonable that respect should be shown to him on account

---

[1] *Analogy of Nature and Grace*, by the Rev. C. Pritchard, President of the Royal Astronomical Society, p. 89.

of what another has done for him, and on the ground of the adequate merit of the one who has thus intervened. He understands that this merit becomes his, and that in regard to his liability to punishment another has been substituted to bear this in his place. This is all natural, and perceived at once without difficulty. The narratives of conversions from among the heathen prove all this. The expectations of the world are very precious to those who are waiting in darkness, and the realisation will be an invaluable memory throughout eternity.

The power of personal attraction is the most commonly known, and the most generally eulogised of all our emotions—love. Our love to God springs at once from the perception that God loves us; *so* loved us, as to give His Son for us. The Holy Spirit moves along this line, our wills are therein and thereby brought into accord with the Divine will, and we become new creatures in Christ Jesus. The Great Sacrifice, received by faith, mollifies the heart of man, by its natural aptitude to produce this effect. We see first that reconciliation is possible, and then that it has been made.

There have been many events in the history of the world besides the crucifixion which have called forth the admiration and enthusiasm of the people; but all such excitements, save this one, after more or less lapse of time, have faded into insignificance. The resulting gratitude and love from this, has been, and still is, displayed and experienced by thousands of every tribe and nation and tongue. It is ever "the true and living way." No satisfactory theory has ever been invented to account for the rapid progress of

Christianity in the world, save that which attributes it to the exact adaptation of its provisions to human nature as it is.

No heathen religion can claim for itself what we have shown to be a characteristic of the religion of Christ, for no pagan utterance or provision has successfully appealed to people of every kind. There is not amidst the vast labyrinth of heathen mythology any truth of universal application to the mind and heart of man. Nor is this exemplified only in rude or abject natures, but it obtains with equal force in the case of the most cultured and scholarly. As Professor Radford Thomson puts it: 'The conscience of the most intelligent, and of those most earnestly striving after goodness, finds repose and satisfaction in the Gospel of pardon and acceptance through Jesus Christ, in whose incarnation and sacrifice the Divine Governor appears supremely just, and at the same time supremely gracious, condemning sin, and absolving the repentant and believing sinner.'[1]

Speaking of Christian missionaries, Dr. Livingstone says: 'Missionaries do not live before their time. Their great idea of converting the world to Christ is no chimera—it is Divine—Christianity will triumph. It is equal to all it has to perform. No mission has yet been an entire failure.' This is the more deserving of note as we remember that every nationality has set up some model for admiration, some ideal of virtue and beauty; but these local goals are radically defective, different in each case, although in some instances they have been supported by the sentiments of successive generations. The moral as

[1] *Present Day Tracts* ii. 40.

well as the physical beauty admired and expressed by the Egyptians, the Greeks, and the Chinese, for instance, are wholly different from each other.

But the appreciation of the Gospel becomes native to the whole world. As Christ is the ideal type of the whole human race, so His salvation is the great deliverance which the literature of all people points to with desire.

'If, in the wisdom of the Godhead, such a way could be devised by which God Himself could save the soul from the consequences of its guilt—by which He Himself could in some way suffer and make self-denials for its good; and by His own interposition open a way for the soul to recover from its lost and condemned condition, then the result would follow inevitably, that every one of the human family who had been led to see and feel his guilty condition before God, and who believed in God thus manifesting Himself to rescue his soul from spiritual death—every one thus believing would, from the necessities of his nature, be led to love God, his Saviour; and mark, the greater the self-denial and the suffering on the part of the Saviour, in ransoming the soul, the stronger would be the affection felt for Him.'[1]

'I believe,' says Bacon in his *Confession of Faith*, 'that at the first the soul of man was not produced by heaven or earth, but was breathed immediately from God. So that the ways and proceedings of God with spirits are not included in nature, that is, in the laws of heaven and earth; but are reserved to the law of His secret will and grace; wherever God worketh still, and resteth not from the work of our redemption,

---

[1] *Philosophy of the Plan of Salvation*, chap. xv.

as He resteth from the work of creation, but continueth working to the end of the world.'

The method of atonement restates and emphasises this conviction, and by giving it a reasonable basis, binds us at once in personal relations to God, and becomes the source and spring of our highest energies, and most active holiness. This reflex action of love is the real missing link in the condition of fallen humanity. It is grounded on the moral law, of which, in the lofty language of Hooker, it may be said that 'Her seat is the bosom of God, her voice the harmony of the world.' In the Atonement we see, without reasoning about it, the nature of the thoughts and intentions of the Divine Ruler towards us.

The witty and profligate Lord Rochester, when the pain and enforced solitude of the illness that preceded his death gave him time and opportunity for calmly considering the claims of the religion which he had opposed and scorned, disclosed to Bishop Burnet the final conclusions of his mind in conversations which the bishop recorded. He relates of the earl,

'He said he was now persuaded both of the truth of Christianity, and of the power of inward grace, of which he gave me this strange account: he said Mr. Parsons, in order to his conviction, read to him Isaiah liii., and compared that with the history of our Saviour's passion, that he might there see a prophecy concerning it, written many ages before it was done; which the Jews that blasphemed Jesus Christ still kept in their hands, as a book divinely inspired.

'He said to me that as he heard it read, he felt an inward force upon him, which did so enlighten his mind and convince him, that he could resist it no longer, for the words had an authority which did shoot like rays and beams in his mind, so that he was not only convinced by the reasonings he had about it, which satisfied his understanding, but by a power which did so effectually constrain him, that he did ever after as firmly believe in his Saviour as if he had seen Him in the clouds. He had made it to be read so often to him, that he had got it by heart, and went through a great part of it, in discourse with me, with a sort of heavenly pleasure, giving me his reflections on it.'

The brightness of spiritual life which characterises such experiences as these forms a complete contrast to the gloom which envelops all agnosticism and the religion of mere humanity.

We may apostrophise the latter with Bonar :

> Era of myth and mystery, how blank
> For truth and goodness have your ages been !
> Ye fabled deities, what have you done
> To sweeten or dry up the turbid flood
> Of terrene ill ? Ah ! never have ye gone
> Down to the solemn depths of human conscience,
> To calm the tempest that was raging there ;
> No burdens have ye borne, no wrinkles smoothed
> Upon the furrowed front of earthly care,
> Dumb as your statues, and as cold.

Nor is it only to the testimony of individual minds that we can appeal. The united judgment of the ablest men of different communions and ages is in favour of the congruity of the Gospel to the nature and needs of men at large. We adduce two instances as parallel or representative :—

THE COUNCIL OF TRENT. *Roman Church*, A.D. 1563.	THE WESTMINSTER ASSEMBLY. *Protestant Church*, A.D. 1643.
Christ, who, whilst we were enemies, for the love alone which He had for us, by His suffering on the Cross, procured meritoriously our justification, and made satisfaction to the Father for us.	The Lord Jesus, by His perfect obedience and sacrifice of Himself, which He, through the Eternal Spirit, once offered up unto God, hath fully satisfied the justice of His Father, and purchased, not only reconciliation, but an everlasting inheritance in the kingdom of heaven, for all those whom the Father hath given unto Him. *Westminster Confession*, chap. viii., sect. 5.

Philosophers resent the dogma of theologians which affirms that there may be something in the action of men's minds independent of any evidence which takes them out of and beyond the realm of ascertained earthly cause and effect, and requires a Divine providence as a factor. They, on the contrary, affirm the absolute dependence of effect upon ordinary causes, and their consequent uniformity, independent of chance on the one hand, and of supernatural interference on the other. But surely the only theory which embraces all the facts is that, which, while admitting uniformity and second causes to be common methods, yet affirms that the Divine Governor stills retains an immediate rule in the spirits of men, and exercises it through the medium of the intellect and feelings, so giving a new direction to the forces of the inner life.

Analyse and classify as you will all the phenomena

of Christian society, then separate whatever is accountable on the calculations of self-interest, there still remains a residuum insoluble by our earth-born chemistry, a *force majeure*, the power of the Highest, manifesting itself in the spiritual world of faith and love. Well does old Sibbes say: 'To bring God and the soul together by trusting on Him must be effected by the mighty power of God raising up the soul to Himself, to lay hold upon the glorious power, goodness, and other excellences that are in Him. God is not only the object, but the working cause of our trust.'[1]

The reception of the truth opens up at once and for ever a new relationship with God, and a new connection with all men everywhere who are relying on Jesus Christ.

The family tie, extended to the clan or to the community, has produced enormous sacrifices in all parts of the world; but from its nature it weakens as it extends, and cannot be a universal ground of appeal. The personal tie has produced heroic instances of devotion amongst all tribes and peoples, and has raised armies, and led to conquests. But the world has not any hero whose qualities or actions at all times were worthy of world-wide enthusiasm; and it has been the dream and hope of humanity through all the ages to find some such one. It is the peculiar excellence of Christianity that what 'the law could not do,' what natural society could not evolve, Christ has effected. There is no true unity for the human race save in Christ. It is the manifestation of this which is the successful theme of the missionary.

The love of Jesus is at the same time the greatest

---

[1] *Soul's Conflict*, chap. xx.

individual force known to our moral nature, and its greatest social power.

The attachment of affection to the person of Christ as a Divine Saviour, by the believer in Him becomes at once the master principle. The love of family, of friends, of country grows up under its sheltering influence; it is like the vine and the branches, 'Without Me ye can do nothing.' A passionate personal devotion to a Divine model is evidently the hope and happiness of the world. It restores order in the chaos of the soul, and makes self-sacrifice a natural and masterful law.

Anselm, when treating of the satisfaction made by Christ on behalf of the sinner, and accepted by God, says: 'The whole world can hear nothing more remarkable, nothing more comforting nothing more desirable. For my part, I take such confidence from it, that I cannot tell you with what joy my heart is gladdened.'

> What in all ages, everywhere, hath been
> By all believed, although unfelt, unseen
> By outward sense, accept; nor ask for more
> Than patriarch, saint, or prophet held of yore.
> Not on cold logic rests the Christian plan—
> It is ingrafted in the heart of man.
>
> J. HERMAN MERIVALE.

In recalling such instances from autobiographies of the past we may well exclaim :—

> 'Joy to the world, the Lord is come,
> Let earth receive her King.
> Let every heart prepare Him room,
> And heaven and nature sing.'

On a review of the facts we may briefly make the following deductions.

I. The variances which have been produced by external circumstances in the appearance and character of the races of mankind, in the course of time, have not affected their susceptibility to the religion of Christ.

II. We therefore infer that the progress of discovery will not disclose the existence of any race or person, to whom the Gospel is not suited.

III. Evolution, or future development, cannot affect the object or subject of the missionary. We may safely consider that he will encounter in the coming time only facts and forces which have been repeatedly met in the past, and uniformly conquered by the Gospel all down the Christian ages. The motto on the banner of the cross is still '*In hoc signo vinces.*'

IV. This consideration is absolutely fatal to the dismal agnosticism which gathers round the purely intellectual consideration of things. We are framed to enjoy more than mere knowledge; the force of emotion brings us into sympathy with Divine purpose and plan. The horizon of love which extends around the Christian's new view is practically illimitable. So far from saying with Mr. Herbert Spencer that nothing can be known in its *essence*, we are constantly learning more of the essence of a love which passeth knowledge. We experience continual surprises, and enjoy constantly fresh delights.

V. From the fall of man to the present time the work of redemption has been carried on by communications of the Spirit of God, mostly in connection with revealed truth.

What we have attempted to prove is, that the susceptibility which God, in His infinite wisdom has seen fit to make a prerequisite to the reception of spiritual saving truth, may be found in men of every race under heaven, and that there is therefore the fullest warrant for the universal preaching of the Gospel. We are acting in an orderly, that is to say, in a scientific manner, according to recorded knowledge, in promoting Christian missions, and fulfilling the glorious promise of our Lord, ' And this Gospel of the Kingdom shall be preached in all the world, for a witness unto all nations.'[1]

In thus listening to the many varying voices of the Christian ages, may we not even now hear them blending in harmony, unitedly ' saying with a loud voice, Worthy is the Lamb that was slain, to receive power, and riches, and wisdom, and strength, and glory, and honour and blessing.'[2] Our thoughts carry us forward to the last great scene in the history of man's redemption, when the drama of this world shall come to its close, and the curtain shall rise upon eternity. ' After this I beheld, and, lo, a great multitude which no man could number, of all nations, and kindreds, and people

---

[1] Matt. xxiv. 14.   [2] Rev. v. 12.

and tongues, stood before the throne, and before the Lamb, clothed with white robes, and palms in their hands, and cried with a loud voice, saying, Salvation to our God which sitteth upon the throne, and unto the Lamb.'[1]

> 'Immortal honour, endless fame,
> Attend the Almighty Father's name:
> Let God the Son be glorified,
> Who for lost man's redemption died:
> And equal adoration be,
> Eternal Comforter, to Thee.'

[1] Rev. vii. 9.

THE END.

The Religious Tract Society's
LIST OF BOOKS.

The Religious Tract Society Publishes Several Thousands of Books for all readers, at all prices, from One Farthing to One Guinea. This List gives the Titles of many that are suitable for presentation, but the following Catalogues, containing full Lists of the Society's Publications, are also issued, and will be forwarded, Post Free, on application to The Secretaries, 56, Paternoster Row, E.C. :—

General Catalogue of Books.	Books for Circulating Libraries.
Classified List of General Literature.	Tracts, Handbills, Leaflets.
Classified List of Tracts.	Publications in various Languages.
Illustrated Catalogue of Gift Books.	Diagrams and Pictures for Lecturers.

CHIEF OFFICE: 56, Paternoster Row, London.

A large variety of Presentation Books at all prices may be inspected at the Retail Depôts.

London: 65, St. Paul's Churchyard (*Opposite the Northern Entrance to the Cathedral*), and 164, Piccadilly.

Liverpool: 18, Slater Street. Manchester: 100, Corporation Street. Brighton: 31, Western Road.

THE RELIGIOUS TRACT SOCIETY'S LIST.

Price Twenty-five Shillings. *(Just published.)*

WALKS IN PALESTINE. The letterpress by HENRY A. HARPER. Illustrated by twenty-four Photogravures from Photographs taken by C. V. SHADBOLT, Esq. Royal 4to. 25s. bevelled boards, gilt edges.

This volume forms a superb gift-book and souvenir of the Holy Land. Mr. Shadbolt's photographs are of the highest merit, and they have been most beautifully reproduced by Messrs. Annan & Swan. The letterpress is from the pen of Mr. Harper, who has lived for years in Palestine, and is familiar with every spot shown in the illustrations. As a presentation volume this will hold its own against any of the same class that have been issued from the press.

One Guinea.

The Lands of Scripture.—Illustrated by Pen and Pencil. Containing "Those Holy Fields" and "The Land of the Pharaohs," by the Rev. S. MANNING, LL.D.; and "Pictures from Bible Lands," by the Rev. S. G. GREEN, D.D. Imperial 8vo. 21s. handsomely bound in cloth gilt.

This elegantly bound and profusely illustrated volume forms a very suitable Presentation Book to a Minister, Sunday-school Superintendent, or Teacher. It gives, in a concise and interesting form, a large amount of information about the places mentioned in Scripture, such as would prove of great service to every Bible Student.

Sixteen Shillings Each.

Pioneering in New Guinea.	Edersheim's Bible History.
By JAMES CHALMERS, of New Guinea. Map and Illustrations. 16s. cloth.	Complete in four vols. 16s. the set, cloth boards.

Half-a-Guinea.

A Handsome Gift Book for Christmas, Birthdays, Weddings, Partings, &c., or for a School Prize.

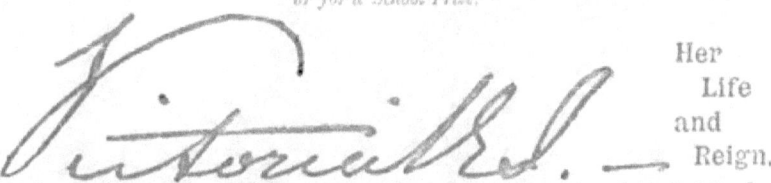

Her Life and Reign.

By Dr. MACAULAY, Author of "Sea Pictures," "Luther Anecdotes," "Gordon Anecdotes," etc. With Five Portraits of the Queen, and Sixty Engravings by Edward Whymper and others. Small Quarto, 10s. 6d. cloth, gilt edges.

"The author's endeavour has been to recall those qualities in the personal character of the Queen and the incidents in her life which have most endeared her to her people."—*Illustrated London News.*

"There is much more of the 'life' than of the 'reign,' the author having devoted most of his attention to the Queen in her domestic relations."—*N.B. Daily Mail.*

"Dr. Macaulay, with his practised pen, tells the story well, with just as much reference to history as the circumstances require."—*Spectator.*

"A very acceptable gift-book."—*Stamford Mercury.*

"It is a beautifully printed and very prettily illustrated volume, and is admirable in tone and feeling."—*Athenæum.*

Ten Shillings.

Historic Landmarks in the Christian Centuries. By RICHARD HEATH. With Eighty-four Illustrations. Quarto. 10s. handsome cloth gilt.

"Calculated at once to give a bird's-eye view of history, and to impress its most important events strongly on the memory."—*Standard.*

"Will prove a most acceptable gift-book."—*Western Morning News.*

THE RELIGIOUS TRACT SOCIETY'S LIST.

Reduced from]   BLESSING THE BOATS.   ["Irish Pictures," see next page.

56 PATERNOSTER ROW, LONDON; and of all Booksellers.

Eight Shillings Each.

THE PEN AND PENCIL SERIES OF
ILLUSTRATED TABLE BOOKS.

Imperial 8vo (size of page, 11 by 7½ inches), beautifully Illustrated, and printed on superior paper, price 8s. in handsome cloth, gilt edges; or 25s. each in morocco, elegant.

JUST PUBLISHED, THE NEW VOLUME OF THIS SERIES.

IRISH PICTURES.
Drawn with Pen and Pencil.

By RICHARD LOVETT, M.A., Author of "Norwegian Pictures," "Pictures from Holland," etc. With a Map and over one hundred Illustrations from Sketches and Photographs, engraved by EDWARD WHYMPER, R. and E. TAYLOR, and others. Imperial 16mo. 8s. cloth boards, gilt edges.

Pictures from Holland. Drawn with Pen and Pencil. By RICHARD LOVETT, M.A. With one hundred and forty Illustrations.

The Land of the Pharaohs. Illustrated. By Dr. MANNING. New Edition, with many new Engravings.

American Pictures by Pen and Pencil. By the Rev. Dr. MANNING.

Sea Pictures by Pen and Pencil. By Dr. MACAULAY.

English Pictures by Pen and Pencil. By Dr. MANNING.

French Pictures by Pen and Pencil. By Dr. GREEN.

Indian Pictures by Pen and Pencil. By WILLIAM URWICK, M.A.

Italian Pictures by Pen and Pencil. By Dr. MANNING.

Canadian Pictures. By the MARQUIS OF LORNE.

Australian Pictures by Pen and Pencil. By HOWARD WILLOUGHBY.

Norwegian Pictures by Pen and Pencil. By RICHARD LOVETT, M.A.

Pictures from Bible Lands. By Dr. GREEN.

Pictures from the German Fatherland by Pen and Pencil. By Dr. GREEN.

Scottish Pictures by Pen and Pencil. By Dr. GREEN.

Swiss Pictures by Pen and Pencil. By Dr. MANNING.

"Those Holy Fields:" Palestine Illustrated by Pen and Pencil. By Dr. MANNING.

Eight Shillings Each.

The History of the Jews, from the War with Rome to the Present Time. By the Rev. H. C. ADAMS, M.A., Vicar of Old Shoreham, Author of "Wykehamica," "Schoolboy Honour," etc. Illustrated. 8vo. 8s. cloth boards.

John Wycliffe and his English Precursors. By Professor LECHLER, D.D., of the University of Leipsic. Translated from the German by PETER LORIMER, D.D. New Edition, very carefully Revised, by S. G. GREEN, D.D. Portrait and Illustrations. 8s. cloth boards.

The Spanish Reformers, their Memories and Dwelling Places. Illustrated. By Dr. STOUGHTON. 8s. cloth gilt.

Homes and Haunts of Luther. By Dr. STOUGHTON. Illustrated. 8s. cloth gilt.

Footprints of Italian Reformers. By Dr. STOUGHTON. Beautifully Illustrated. Cloth gilt, 8s.

William Tyndale. A Biography. A contribution to the History of the English Bible. By the Rev. R. DEMAUS, M.A. New Edition, carefully revised. 8vo. 8s. cloth boards.

Seven and Sixpence Each.

The Midnight Sky. Familiar Notes on the Stars and Planets. By EDWIN DUNKIN, F.R.S., of the Royal Observatory, Greenwich. With thirty-two Star Maps and numerous other Illustrations. Imp. 8vo. 7s. 6d. cloth; 9s. extra boards, with gilt edges.

Biblical Encyclopædia; or, Dictionary of Eastern Antiquities, Geography, Natural History, Sacred Annals and Biography, Theology, and Biblical Literature. By Dr. EADIE. Maps and Illustrations. 8vo. 7s. 6d. cloth, 10s. 6d. half bound, 12s. 6d. calf, 13s. 6d. morocco.

THE RELIGIOUS TRACT SOCIETY'S LIST.

Eight Shilling Books for Young People.

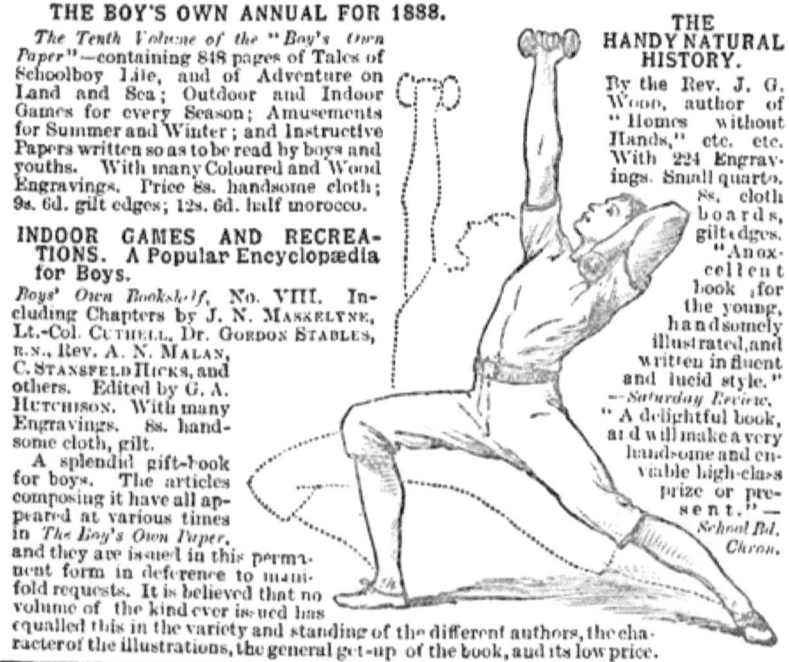

THE GIRL'S OWN ANNUAL FOR 1888.

The Ninth Volume of the "Girl's Own Paper"—containing 848 pages of interesting and useful reading. Stories by popular writers; Music by eminent composers; Practical Papers for young Housekeepers; Medical Papers by a well-known practitioner; Needlework, plain and fancy; Helpful Papers for Christian Girls; Papers on Reasonable and Seasonable Dress, etc. etc. Profusely Illustrated. Price 8s. in handsome cloth; 9s. 6d. with gilt edges; 12s. 6d. half morocco.

THE GIRL'S OWN INDOOR BOOK.

Edited by CHARLES PETERS. With over one hundred and fifty illustrations. Quarto. 8s. cloth boards, gilt edges.

Containing practical helps to Girls in all matters relating to their material comfort and moral well-being, by the Author of "How to be Happy though Married," Dora de Blaquiere, Dora Hope, Marie Karger, Lady Macfarren, Lady Lindsay, Ernst Pauer, Sir John Stainer, The Hon. Victoria Grosvenor, John C. Staples, Canon Fleming, "Medicus," Ruth Lamb, Sophia Caulfeild, and many others.

THE BOY'S OWN ANNUAL FOR 1888.

The Tenth Volume of the "Boy's Own Paper"—containing 848 pages of Tales of Schoolboy Life, and of Adventure on Land and Sea; Outdoor and Indoor Games for every Season; Amusements for Summer and Winter; and Instructive Papers written so as to be read by boys and youths. With many Coloured and Wood Engravings. Price 8s. handsome cloth; 9s. 6d. gilt edges; 12s. 6d. half morocco.

INDOOR GAMES AND RECREATIONS. A Popular Encyclopædia for Boys.

Boys' Own Bookshelf, No. VIII. Including Chapters by J. N. MASKELYNE, Lt.-Col. CUTHELL, Dr. GORDON STABLES, R.N., Rev. A. N. MALAN, C. STANSFELD HICKS, and others. Edited by G. A. HUTCHISON. With many Engravings. 8s. handsome cloth, gilt.

A splendid gift-book for boys. The articles composing it have all appeared at various times in The Boy's Own Paper, and they are issued in this permanent form in deference to manifold requests. It is believed that no volume of the kind ever issued has equalled this in the variety and standing of the different authors, the character of the illustrations, the general get-up of the book, and its low price.

THE HANDY NATURAL HISTORY.

By the Rev. J. G. WOOD, author of "Homes without Hands," etc. etc. With 224 Engravings. Small quarto. 8s. cloth boards, gilt edges.

"An excellent book for the young, handsomely illustrated, and written in fluent and lucid style."—Saturday Review.

"A delightful book, and will make a very handsome and enviable high-class prize or present."—School Bd. Chron.

56, PATERNOSTER ROW, LONDON; and of all Booksellers. 5

THE RELIGIOUS TRACT SOCIETY'S LIST.

Seven Shillings Each.

The Leisure Hour
ANNUAL VOLUME FOR 1888.

"Behold in these what leisure hours demand, Amusement and true knowledge hand in hand."

THE VOLUME FOR 1888 of this Family Journal of Instruction and Recreation—contains 860 pages of interesting reading, with numerous Illustrations by Eminent Artists. It forms a handsome Book for Presentation, and an appropriate and instructive volume for a School or College Prize. Price 7s. in cloth boards; 8s. 6d. extra boards, gilt edges; 10s. 6d. half-bound in calf.

The Sunday at Home
ANNUAL VOLUME FOR 1888.

The Illustrated Family Magazine for Sabbath Reading.

THIS VOLUME FOR 1888 forms a very suitable Book for Presentation. It contains 828 pages, with a great variety of Interesting and Instructive Sabbath Reading for every Member of the Family. It is profusely illustrated by Coloured and Wood Engravings. Price 7s. cloth boards; 8s. 6d. extra boards, gilt edges; 10s. 6d. half-bound in calf.

Random Truths in Common Things. Occasional Papers from my Study Chair. By the Rev. J. R. VERNON, M.A., Author of "The Harvest of a Quiet Eye." Illustrations. 7s. cloth gilt.

"It seems even better than 'The Harvest of a Quiet Eye.'"—*Mr. Ruskin.*
"Should be placed next to Wordsworth on every student's bookshelf."—*Standard.*

Six Shillings Each.

The Crown of Flowers. Poems and Pictures from "The Girl's Own Paper." 6s. handsomely bound.

Winter Pictures. By Poet and Artist. An elegant book, most appropriate for a Christmas or New Year's Gift. Profusely illustrated by EDWARD WHYMPER. Quarto. 6s. cloth boards, gilt.

Storyland. A Book for Children. By SYDNEY GREY. With Thirty-two Coloured Illustrations by ROBERT BARNES. Quarto. 6s. handsomely bound in coloured paper boards.

Work and Adventure in New Guinea, 1877 to 1885. By JAMES CHALMERS, of Port Moresby, and W. WYATT GILL, B.A. With Illustrations. Crown 8vo. 6s. cloth.

Ingleside and Wayside Musings. A companion volume to "The Harvest of a Quiet Eye." 6s. cloth gilt.

In Southern India. By Mrs. MURRAY MITCHELL, Author of "In India, a Missionary's Wife among the Wild Tribes of South Bengal," etc. Map and Illustrations. Crown 8vo. 6s. cloth boards.

Five Shillings Each.

Ants and their Ways. By the Rev. W. FARREN WHITE, M.A. With numerous Illustrations, and a Complete List of Genera and Species of the British Ants. 5s. cloth boards.

The Honey Bee: its Nature, Homes, and Products. By W. H. HARRIS, B.A., B.SC. With Eighty-two Illustrations. 5s. cloth.

Chrysostom: His Life and Times. By Rev. R. WHELER BUSH, M.A., F.R.G.S. Crown 8vo. 5s. cloth.

Edersheim's The Temple in the Time of Christ. 5s. cloth gilt.

Edersheim's Jewish Life in the Time of Christ. 5s. cloth gilt.

Every-day Life in China; or, Scenes along River and Road in the Celestial Empire. By EDWIN JOSHUA DUKES. With Illustrations. 5s. cloth.

Gospel Ethnology. By S. R. PATTISON, F.G.S., Author of "The Religious Topography of England," etc. With Illustrations. 5s. cloth.

Past and Present in the East. By the Rev. HARRY JONES, M.A., Prebendary of St. Paul's Cathedral. With Engravings. 5s. cloth, gilt.

Glimpses of Maori Land. By A. R. BUTLER. Illustrated. Crown 8vo. 5s. cloth.

Jottings from the Pacific. By the Rev. W. WYATT GILL, B.A. Illustrated. Crown 8vo. 5s. cloth.

Hanna's Our Lord's Life on Earth. 5s. cloth.

The Life of Jesus Christ the Saviour, for Young People. By Mrs. S. WATSON. With Engravings. Crown 8vo. 5s. cloth.

6 *56, PATERNOSTER ROW, LONDON; and of all Booksellers.*

THE RELIGIOUS TRACT SOCIETY'S LIST.

The Cabinet Room at Downing Street.
Reduced from "The Leisure Hour" Volume for 1888.

A handsome gift book, containing, among other interesting papers and stories, GREAT GRANDMAMMA SEVERN. By Leslie Keith.—THE QUEEN'S HOMES: Osborne, Balmoral, Windsor, Buckingham Palace, Frogmore, Kensington, etc. By C. E. Pascoe.—PRINCESS SARAH. By J. S. Winter.—VOICES FROM THE HIGHWAYS AND HEDGES. By I. F. Mayo.—THE STORY OF THE ENGLISH SHIRES. By Canon Creighton.—NORWAY FROM THE SEA. By Harry Jones, M.A.—MY BEST SHIPMATE: A Sea Officer's Reminiscence. By G. Cupples. And a host of other Shorter Sketches and Papers, with a profusion of Illustrations. 7s. handsome cloth; 8s. 6d. extra cloth, gilt; 10s. 6d. half calf.

56, *PATERNOSTER ROW, LONDON; and of all Booksellers.*

Five-Shilling Story Books.
(See also books by E. EVERETT GREEN on p. 9.)

Ernest Hepburn; or, Revenge and Forgiveness. By H. C. ADAMS, M.A., Vicar of Old Shoreham. Author of "Schoolboy Honour," etc. Illustrated by E. WHYMPER. Crown 8vo. 5s. cloth boards.

In a Jesuit Net. A Story of the Time of Louis XIV. By H. C. COAPE, Author of "The Château de Louard," etc. Illustrated by E. WHYMPER. Cr. 8vo. 5s. cloth boards.

The Château de Louard; or, The Friends and Foes of Isaac Homel. A Story of France at the period of the Revocation of the Edict of Nantes. By H. C. COAPE. Illustrated by E. WHYMPER. Crown 8vo. 5s. cloth.

Count Renneberg's Treason. A Tale of the Siege of Steenwick. By HARRIET E. BURCH. Illustrated. Crown 8vo. 5s. cloth.

The Fifth Form at St. Dominics. By TALBOT BAINES REED, Author of "Adventures of a Three-Guinea Watch," etc. Illustrated. 5s. cloth.

Young Sir Richard. By H. FREDERICK CHARLES, Author of "The Doctor's Experiment," "Under Fire," etc. Illustrations by E. WHYMPER. Crown 8vo. 5s. cloth boards.

Untrue to his Trust. A Story of Life and Adventure in Charles the Second's Time. By HENRY JOHNSON. Illustrated. 5s. cloth, gilt edges.

The Doctor's Experiment. A Story for Boys. By the Author of "Under Fire." With Illustrations. Imperial 16mo. 5s. cloth, gilt edges.

The Captain's Story of Life in Jamaica. With Illustrations by JOHN GILBERT. Imperial 16mo. 5s. cloth boards, gilt edges.

BY HESBA STRETTON,
Author of "Jessica's First Prayer," &c.

Cobwebs and Cables. Illustrated. 5s. cloth gilt.

BY W. H. G. KINGSTON.

The Two Voyages; or, Midnight and Daylight. Illustrated. 5s. cloth, gilt edges.

A Yacht Voyage Round England. Profusely Illustrated. 5s. cloth, gilt edges.

The Golden Grasshopper: a Tale founded on events in the days of Sir Thomas Gresham. With Illustrations. 5s. cloth, gilt edges.

Captain Cook: his Life, Voyages, and Discoveries. With Illustrations. 5s. cloth, gilt edges.

The Franklins. By GEORGE E. SARGENT, Author of "The Story of a City Arab," etc. With Illustrations. Imperial 16mo. 5s. cloth, gilt.

The Realm of the Ice King: a Book of Arctic Discovery and Adventure. New Edition, revised to present date. With Illustrations. 5s. cloth, gilt edges.

Without Intending It; or, John Tincroft, Bachelor and Benedict. By G. E. SARGENT. 5s. cloth gilt.

Straight to the Mark. A Story for Old and Young. By the Rev. T. S. MILLINGTON, M.A., Author of "Boy and Man," etc. Illustrated. Imperial 16mo. 5s. cloth, gilt edges.

The Old Manuscript; or, Anaise Robineau's History. A Tale of the Huguenots in La Vendée. By BLANCHE M. MOGGRIDGE. With Five Illustrations. Crown 8vo. 5s. cloth.

Four Shillings Each.

The Golden Diary of Heart Converse with Jesus in the Book of Psalms. Arranged for every Sunday in the Year. By Dr. EDERSHEIM. 4s. cloth, gilt.

Tulsipur Fair. Glimpses of Missionary Life in India. For Young People. By the Rev. B. H. BADLEY, M.A. Numerous Engravings. 4s. cloth gilt.

Chapters on Every-day Things; or, Histories and Marvels in Common Life. Illustrated. 4s. cloth, gilt edges.

My Coloured Picture Story-Book. With Twenty-four full-page coloured Pictures, and forty Vignettes. Quarto. 4s. handsome cloth gilt.

Boy and Man. A Story for Old and Young. By the Rev. T. S. Millington, M.A., Illustrated. 4s. cloth gilt.

Shadows. By Mrs. O. F. WALTON, Author of "Christie's Old Organ," etc. 4s. cloth gilt.

The Children of India. Written for the Children of England by one of their Friends. 4s. cloth gilt.

Under Fire: being the Story of a Boy's Battles against Himself and other Enemies. 4s. cloth gilt.

Tales of Three Centuries. By Madame GUIZOT DE WITT. 4s. cloth gilt.

Bible Stories and Pictures. With 24 Coloured page Pictures and 40 Vignettes. 4s. cloth gilt.

FIVE SHILLING STORIES BY E. EVERETT GREEN.

Two Enthusiasts. Illustrated by EDWARD WHYMPER. 5s. cloth (*See Engraving*.)
Joint Guardians. Illustrated. Crown 8vo. 5s. cloth boards.
Barbara's Brothers. Illustrated. Crown 8vo. 5s. cloth boards.

The Head of the House. With Illustrations. Crown 8vo. 5s. cloth.
Lenore Annandale's Story. With Illustrations. 5s. cloth.
The Mistress of Lydgate Priory; or, The Story of a Long Life. Illustrated. Crown 8vo. 5s. cloth.

Three Shillings and Sixpence each.

The Happiest Half-Hour; or, Sunday Talks with Children. By FREDERICK LANGBRIDGE, M.A., Author of "Sent Back by the Angels," "Poor Folks' Lives," etc. With many illustrations. Small quarto. 3s. 6d. cloth boards, gilt edges.

Through Fire and Through Water. A Story of Adventure and Peril. By T. S. MILLINGTON, Author of "A Great Mistake," "Straight to the Mark," etc. Boys' Own Bookshelf, No. VI. Illustrated. Crown 8vo. 3s. 6d. bevelled boards.

Harold, the Boy Earl. A Story of Old England. By J. F. HODGETTS, Author of "Edric the Norseman," etc. Boys' Own Bookshelf, No. VII. Illustrated. Crown 8vo. 3s. 6d. cloth boards.

Mrs. Morse's Girls. A Story of American Sunday School Life. Illustrated. Crown 8vo. 3s. 6d. cloth boards, gilt edges.

Drake and the Dons; or, Stirring Tales of Armada Times. Edited and arranged by RICHARD LOVETT, M.A. With Portraits, Maps, and Illustrations. Crown 8vo. 3s. 6d., cloth boards, gilt edges.

The Heroines of Haarlem. Adapted from the French of Madame de Witt. By HARRIETTE E. BURCH, Author of "Count Renneberg's Treason." With many Illustrations. 3s. 6d. cloth, gilt edges.

Grace Trevelyan; or, Led into Light. By Mrs. COOTE, Author of "The Sure Harvest," "The First Gift," etc. Illustrated. 3s. 6d. cloth boards, gilt edges.

Joyce Graham's History; or, Overcoming Evil with Good. By N. A. GOWRING. Illustrated. 3s. 6d. cloth.

Bede's Charity. By HESBA STRETTON, Author of "Jessica's First Prayer," etc. Illustrated. 3s. 6d. cloth gilt.

Carola. By HESBA STRETTON. Illustrated. 3s. 6d. cloth.

Adventures of a Three Guinea Watch. By TALBOT BAINES REED. Boys' Own Bookshelf, No. I. With Illustrations. 3s. 6d. cloth.

A Great Mistake. A Tale of Adventure. By T. S. MILLINGTON. With many Illustrations. Small quarto. Boys' Own Bookshelf, Vol. IV. 3s. 6d. cloth boards.

Esther. By ROSA NOUCHETTE CAREY. Imperial 16mo. Girls' Own Bookshelf, Vol. VIII. 3s. 6d. cloth gilt.

His Masters. A Story of School Life Forty Years Ago. By S. S. PUGH, Author of "Max Victor," etc. With Illustrations. Imperial 16mo. 3s. 6d. cloth, gilt edges.

A Child without a Name. By EVELYN EVERETT GREEN, Author of "Lenore Annandale's Story," etc. Illustrated. 3s. 6d. cloth, gilt edges.

Seven Years for Rachel. By ANNE BEALE. Illustrated. 3s. 6d. cloth gilt.

Sunflowers. A Story of To-day. By G. C. GEDGE. With four illustrations. 3s. 6d. cloth.

One Day at a Time. By BLANCHE E. M. GREENE. Illustrated. 3s. 6d. cloth boards.

The Two Crowns. By EGLANTON THORNE. With Illustrations. 3s. 6d. cloth boards.

Ida Nicolari. By EGLANTON THORNE. Illustrated. Crown 8vo. 3s. 6d. cloth boards.

Maddalena, the Waldensian Maiden and her People, given in English by JULIE SUTTER. 3s. 6d. cloth boards.

Reaping the Whirlwind. A Story of Three Lives. 3s. 6d. cloth.

Turning Points; or, Two Years in Maud Vernon's Life. By L. C. SILKE. 3s. 6d. cloth boards.

The Martyr's Victory. A Tale of Danish England. By EMMA LESLIE. With Illustrations. Imperial 16mo. 3s. 6d. cloth gilt.

Another King. By JANET EDEN, Author of "Hester's Home," etc. Illustrated. 3s. 6d. cloth boards.

Three Shillings Each.

Bible Sketches and their Teachings. For Young People. Vol. I. Old Testament. Vol. II. New Testament. By S. G. GREEN, D.D. Revised and enlarged edition, with Maps. In 2 vols. 3s. each, cloth.

Through the Linn; or, Miss Temple's Wards. By AGNES GIBERNE. 3s. cloth.

Illustrated Letters to my Children from the Holy Land. Eastern Manners and Customs Depicted in a Series of Sketches from Life. By HENRY A. HARPER. 3s. cloth boards.

Ethel Graham's Victory. By Mrs. H. B. PAULL. Illustrated. 3s. cloth gilt.

THE RELIGIOUS TRACT SOCIETY'S LIST.

From "All for Number One."

All for Number One; or, Charlie Russell's Ups and Downs. A Story for Boys and Girls. By HENRY JOHNSON, Author of "Untrue to His Trust," etc. Illustrated by E. WHYMPER. Crown 8vo. 3s. 6d. cloth boards, gilt edges.

A well-written story, suitable equally for boys and girls, contrasting cruelty, vain-glory and selfishness in "Old Smythe" with generosity and self-sacrifice in "Skylark" and the other chief characters.

THE RELIGIOUS TRACT SOCIETY'S LIST.

Half-a-Crown Each.

Louisa of Prussia and other Sketches. By Rev. JOHN KELLY. With Portraits and Illustrations. Crown 8vo. 2s. 6d. cloth boards.

Aunt Diana. By ROSA NOUCHETTE CAREY, Author of "Not Like Other Girls," "Esther Cameron's Story," etc. Girl's Own Bookshelf, No. X. Illustrated. 2s. 6d.

Geoffrey Heywood; or, The Right Way. By Mrs. COOPER. Illustrated. 2s. 6d. cloth.

Marching Orders; or, Soldier Bobbie. By LUCY TAYLOR. Illustrated. 2s. 6d. cloth.

Our Little Dot's Annual for 1888. Handsome cloth, gilt edges, 2s. 6d.

Child's Companion Volume for 1888. Extra cloth boards, gilt edges. 2s. 6d.

My Holiday Picture-Book. With Coloured Pictures. 2s. 6d. cloth boards.

Children's Daily Bread. A Picture, Text, and Verse for Every Day of the Year. 2s. 6d. cloth.

Friendly Greetings. Illustrated Readings for the People. Half-yearly volumes for 1888. 2s. 6d. each, cloth. Each complete in itself.

NEW HALF-CROWN SERIES OF STORIES.
Each with 384 pages, Illustrated, and bound in handsome cloth, gilt edges.

The Foster Brothers of Doon. A Tale of the Irish Rebellion of 1798. By the Author of "Cedar Creek."

Cedar Creek. From the Shanty to the Settlement. A Tale of Canadian Life.

Strange Tales of Peril and Adventure.

Remarkable Adventures from Real Life.

The Black Troopers, and other Stories.

Adventures Ashore and Afloat.

Finding Her Place. By HOWE BENNING.

The Mountain Path. By LILY WATSON.

Among the Mongols. By Rev. J. GILMOUR.

Within Sea Walls; or, How the Dutch Kept the Faith. By G. E. SARGENT.

Chronicles of an Old Manor House. By the late G. E. SARGENT.

A Race for Life, and other Tales.

Two Shillings Each.

The Latch-Key. By T. S. MILLINGTON, Author of "A Great Mistake," "Through Fire and through Water," etc. Illustrated. Crown 8vo. 2s. cloth boards.

May. "a Succourer of Many." By Miss A. G. GRAY-JONES. With Illustrations. Crown 8vo. 2s. cloth.

Breaking the Fetters; or, The Last of the Galley Slaves. By EMMA LESLIE. Illustrated. 2s. cloth boards.

Higher Up. By NELLIE HELLIS. Illustrated. 2s. cloth boards.

More than Conqueror; or, A Boy's Temptations. By HARRIETTE E. BURCH. Illustrated. 2s. cloth.

The Fortunes of the Frejhaldts. A Story of Russian Life. By MARY E. ROPES. Illus. 2s. cloth.

Daddy Crips' Waifs. A Tale of Australian Life and Adventure. 2s.

Child's Companion. Vol. 1888. Profusely Illustrated. 2s. cloth.

Our Little Dots. Vol. 1888. Profusely Illustrated. 2s. cloth.

Cricket. By W. G. GRACE, LORD HARRIS, LORD CHARLES RUSSELL, J. PYCROFT, M.A., W. J. GORDON, FRED. GALE, and others. 2s. cloth.

Talkative Friends in Field, Farm, and Forest. By MARY E. ROPES. Profusely Illustrated. Small 4to. 2s. cloth.

Our Pets and Companions: Pictures and Stories Illustrative of Kindness to Animals. By MARY K. MARTIN. Profusely Illustrated. 4to. 2s. cloth.

Pilgrim's Progress. By JOHN BUNYAN. With Coloured Plates. 2s.

The Child's Book of Poetry. 2s.

By HESBA STRETTON.

The Children of Cloverley.
Enoch Roden's Training.
Fern's Hollow.
The Fishers of Derby Haven.
Pilgrim Street. A Story of Manchester Life.
A Thorny Path.

56, *PATERNOSTER ROW, LONDON: and of all Booksellers.*

THE RELIGIOUS TRACT SOCIETY'S LIST.

From "*Hindered and Helped.*"

Hindered and Helped. A Story for Boys. Illustrated. Crown 8vo. 2s. cloth boards.

The experiences of an American family, full of humour, and showing how some of the weak points in the characters of boys and girls may be strengthened, and how the power of the Gospel can transform the heart and life.

56, *PATERNOSTER ROW, LONDON; and of all Booksellers.*

THE RELIGIOUS TRACT SOCIETY'S LIST.

One and Sixpence Each.

Football. By Dr. IRVINE and C. W. ALCOCK. Illustrated. 1s. 6d. cloth.

What to Read at Winter Entertainments. Part I. Verse. Part II. Prose. Edited and arranged by Rev. FREDERICK LANGBRIDGE, M.A. Each crown 8vo. 1s. 6d. cloth boards.

Dolly. A Quiet Story for Quiet People. By M. F. W. Illustrated. Crown 8vo. 1s. 6d. cloth boards.

Every Day. A Story for Sunday Afternoons. By EVELYN R. FARRAR. Illustrated. Crown 8vo. 1s. 6d. cloth boards.

Dorothy Tresilis. A Cornish Tale. By M. M. POLLARD, Author of "Lilla's Experiment," "Only Me," etc. Illustrated. Crown 8vo. 1s. 6d. cloth boards.

Sailor Jack. A Tale of the Southern Seas. By CONSTANCE CROSS, Author of "After Twenty Years," "Stanley's Summer Visit," etc. With Illustrations. Crown 8vo. 1s. 6d. cloth boards.

Life of John Bunyan. With Portrait and Five Illustrations. New and Revised Edition. Crown 8vo. 1s. 6d. cloth boards.

Humpty Dumpty's Silver Bells. A Story illustrating the Lord's Prayer. By M. S. HAYCRAFT. Illustrated by CHARLES FERRIER. Crown 8vo. 1s. 6d. cloth boards.

Dibs. A Story of Young London Life. By JOSEPH JOHNSON. 1s. 6d.

Ralph Trulock's Christmas Roses. By ANNETTE LYSTER. 1s. 6d. cloth.

Bible Work for Little Fingers. 1s. 6d. paper covers.

SUNDAY BOOKS FOR VERY LITTLE CHILDREN.

Sunday Afternoons at Rose Cottage. By Mrs. WATERWORTH. In very large type. Illustrations. Small Quarto. 1s. 6d. cloth gilt.

Listening to Jesus. By the Author of "Walking with Jesus," etc. In very large type. Illustrations. 1s. 6d. cloth gilt.

Child's Companion Annual for 1888. 1s. 6d. In coloured paper boards.

Cottager and Artisan. Volume 1888. 1s. 6d. coloured stiff cover.

Our Little Dot's Annual for 1888. 1s. 6d. coloured paper boards.

Swallow-tails and Skippers. 1s. 6d.

The Great Auk's Eggs. 1s. 6d. cloth.

Tract Magazine Volume 1888. 1s. 6d.

Livingstone Anecdotes. By Dr. MACAULAY. 1s. 6d. cloth.

Luther Anecdotes. By Dr. MACAULAY. 1s. 6d.

Wesley Anecdotes. By JOHN TELFORD. 1s. 6d.

Whitefield Anecdotes. By Dr. MACAULAY. 1s. 6d. cloth.

Wycliffe Anecdotes. By Dr. GREEN. 1s. 6d. cloth.

BY HESBA STRETTON,
Author of "Jessica's First Prayer."

Alone in London. Illustrated. 1s. 6d. cloth.

Cassy. New Edition. Illustrated. 1s. 6d. cloth.

The Crew of the Dolphin. Illustrated. 1s. 6d. cloth.

Friends till Death, and other Stories. Illustrated. 1s. 6d. cloth.

The King's Servants. Illustrated. 1s. 6d.

Little Meg's Children. New Edition. Illustrated. 1s. 6d. cloth.

Lost Gip. Illustrated. 1s. 6d. cloth.

Max Kromer. A Story of the Siege of Strasbourg. 1s. 6d. cloth.

The Storm of Life. Illustrated. 1s. 6d. cloth.

One Shilling Each.

Morning and Evening. Keble's Morning and Evening Hymns. Beautifully illustrated from sketches by J. CLARK, J. H. HIPSLEY, DAVIDSON KNOWLES, JAMES N. LEE, C. J. STANILAND, J. R. WELLS, and C. M. WIMPERIS. Printed in colour by ALFRED COOKE. In a handsome coloured cover, tied with ribbon. Square 16mo. 1s.

Back Streets and London Slums. By FREDERICK HASTINGS, Author of "The Background of Sacred Story," etc. Illustrated. Crown 8vo. 1s. cloth boards.

Picture Stories for Children. With a Picture on every opening, and with letterpress in large type, well printed. Crown 8vo. 1s. attractively bound in cloth boards.

Picture Book for Children. With a Picture on every opening, and with letterpress in large type, well printed. Crown 8vo. 1s. attractively bound in cloth boards.

My Brother's Love. By Mrs. LUCAS-SHADWELL. Illustrated. 1s. cloth boards.

Theodore Winthrop. By Mrs. LODEN-HOFFER. Illustrated. 1s. cloth boards.

BY HESBA STRETTON.

Jessica's First Prayer. New Edition. Illustrated. 1s. cloth.

No Place Like Home. Illustrated. 1s. cloth.

Under the Old Roof. Illustrated. 1s. cloth.

BY MRS. O. F. WALTON.

Christie's Old Organ; or, Home Sweet Home. 1s. cloth.

Little Faith; or, The Child of the Toy-Stall. Illustrated. 1s.

Nobody Loves Me. Illustrated. 1s. cloth.

Poppie's Presents. Illustrated. 1s. cloth.

Taken or Left. Illustrated. 1s. cloth.

Our Gracious Queen: Pictures and Stories from Her Majesty's Life. Profusely Illustrated. 1s. in attractive cloth.

Saved at Sea. Illustrated. 1s. cloth.

One Shilling Each, for Adults.

A series of nearly 100 Illustrated Books, Printed in Clear Type specially for Working People, 1s. each cloth. For List see the Society's GENERAL CATALOGUE.

56, PATERNOSTER ROW, LONDON: and of all Booksellers.

Ninepence Each.

Each with Coloured Frontispiece and Engravings. 9d. cloth boards.

39 **May's Cousin.** By Author of "Reuben Touchett's Granddaughter."
40 **Billy, the Acorn Gatherer.** By FLORENCE E. BURCH.
41 **Banished Family, and the Bohemian Confessor.**
42 **Golden Street;** or, The Fisherman's Orphans. By SIDNEY GREY.
43 **The First of the African Diamonds.** By FRANCES BROWNE.
44 **The Royal Banner;** or, Dragged in the Dust. By EMMA S. PRATT, Author of "Daisy's Trust," "The Eldest of Seven," etc.
45 **Brave Archie.** By the Author of "Sketches and Stories of Life in Italy," etc.
46 **There's a Friend for Little Children,** and Trusty and True. By CHARLOTTE MASON.
47 **Michael the Young Miner.** A Hungarian Story.
48 **Bob's Trials and Tests.** By MARY E. ROPES, Author of "Till the Sugar Melts," etc.
49 **Tim Peglar's Secret;** or, The Wonderful Egg. By Miss TANDY.
50 **Under the Snow.** By the Author of "Heroes and Famous Men of Old," etc.
51 **The Lost Baby.** A Story of the Floods. By EMMA LESLIE.

Sixpence Each.

The "LITTLE DOT" Series. With Coloured Frontispiece. 6d. cloth.

87 **Pretty Miss Violet.**
88 **The Queen's Oak.** By LUCY BYERLEY.
89 **Story of a Yellow Rose.** By JESSE PAGE.
90 **Blacksmith's Daughter.**
91 **Daisy's Trust.** By E. S. PRATT.
92 **The Runaways.** By SIDNEY GREY.
93 **Jack Silverleigh's Temptation.**
94 **May Lynwood.** A Tale of School Life.
95 **Tom's Bennie.** By MARY E. ROPES.
96 **The Captain of the School,** and other Stories
97 **Miss Pris.** By E. A. CAMPBELL.
98 **The Story he was Told;** or, The Adventures of a Tea-cup. By NELLIE HELLIS.
99 **Gerty's Triumph.** A Cornish Story. By M. B. MANWELL.

Fourpence Each.

Illustrated. 4d. cloth boards.

19 **Made on Purpose.** A Story of Russian Life. By SALEM HALL.
20 **The White Rosebud.**
21 **Carl's Secret.**
22 **Made a Man of.**
23 **Winnie's Golden Key;** or, the Right of Way. By JESSIE M. E. SAXBY.
24 **Trapped on the Rocks;** or, Only a Word.
25 **Susie Wood's Charge.** By MARY E. ROPES.
26 **Fisherman Niels.** By Mrs. GEORGE GLADSTONE.
27 **In Golden London;** or, Raised from the Dead. By MARY E. ROPES.
28 **Watchman Halfdan, and his Little Granddaughter.** By Mrs. GEORGE GLADSTONE.

Fourpenny Toy-Books.

Each with Four full-page Coloured Pictures and Six Vignettes. With simple letterpress in large type. 4d. coloured covers.

1 Amy's Birthday Present.
2 The Bible Picture Alphabet.
3 The Busy Farm.
4 The Children of the Bible.
5 Contented Johnnie.
6 Holiday Time in the Country.

3d. Each.

The "Silver Series" of Books for Children. Covers printed in colours on a Silver ground. Eighteen Books, 3d. each.

2d. Each.

"Floral Cover" Series. Each with 48 pages. Illustrated in pretty coloured covers. Eighteen Books, 2d. each.

1d. Each.

Three Packets, containing 12 Penny Books. Each Book with 32 pages in a pretty cover. Packets A, B, C, 1s. each.

Halfpenny and Farthing Books.

Halfpenny Books in packets, each containing Twenty-four Books for Children, with Pictures and Covers. 1s. the packet; also in 6d. packets, each containing Twelve Books.

Farthing Books in packets, each containing Forty-eight 8-page Books, 1s.; or in 6d. packets, each containing Twenty-four Books.

THE RELIGIOUS TRACT SOCIETY'S LIST.

Magazines for Every Household.

SIXPENCE MONTHLY. ONE PENNY WEEKLY.
THE SUNDAY AT HOME.
A FAMILY MAGAZINE FOR SABBATH READING.
THE ANNUAL VOLUME,
With Coloured and numerous other Engravings, 7s. cloth; 8s. 6d. extra cloth, gilt; 10s. 6d. half calf.

NEW SERIES. SIXPENCE MONTHLY.
THE LEISURE HOUR.
A MONTHLY MAGAZINE FOR FAMILY AND GENERAL READING.
THE ANNUAL VOLUME,
Profusely Illustrated, 7s. cloth; 8s. 6d. extra cloth, gilt; 10s. 6d. half calf.

SIXPENCE MONTHLY. ONE PENNY WEEKLY.
THE GIRL'S OWN PAPER.
THE GIRL'S OWN ANNUAL,
8s. handsome cloth; 9s. 6d. cloth, full gilt; 12s. 6d. half morocco.

SIXPENCE MONTHLY. ONE PENNY WEEKLY.
THE BOY'S OWN PAPER.
THE BOY'S OWN ANNUAL,
8s. handsome cloth; 9s. 6d. extra, full gilt; 12s. 6d. half morocco.

ONE PENNY MONTHLY. IN COVER.
THE CHILD'S COMPANION
AND JUVENILE INSTRUCTOR,
A MAGAZINE FOR THE LITTLE FOLKS
THE CHILD'S COMPANION ANNUAL,
1s. 6d. coloured cover, 2s. cloth, 2s. 6d. full gilt.

NEW SERIES. ONE PENNY MONTHLY.
THE COTTAGER & ARTISAN.
THE MAGAZINE FOR WORKING PEOPLE
IN TOWN AND COUNTRY.
THE ANNUAL VOLUME,
Full of large Pictures
1s. 6d. coloured covers, 2s. 6d. cloth boards gilt.

NEW SERIES. ONE PENNY MONTHLY.
THE TRACT MAGAZINE.
FOR HOME READING AND LOCALISATION.
THE ANNUAL VOLUME,
1s. 6d. cloth boards.

FOURPENCE MONTHLY. HALFPENNY WEEKLY.
FRIENDLY GREETINGS.
ILLUSTRATED READINGS FOR THE PEOPLE.
THE HALF-YEARLY VOLUMES,
Each complete in itself, and Profusely Illustrated, 2s. 6d. cloth boards.

Sixteen Pages. Large Type. Easy Words. One Penny Monthly.
OUR LITTLE DOTS.
The New Illustrated Magazine for Little Boys and Girls.
THE ANNUAL VOLUME,
1s. 6d. attractive coloured cover, 2s. neat cloth, 2s. 6d. handsome cloth, gilt.

LONDON: 56, PATERNOSTER ROW, AND OF ALL NEWSVENDORS.

www.ingramcontent.com/pod-product-compliance
Lightning Source LLC
Chambersburg PA
CBHW031750230426
43669CB00007B/567